SPECTACULAR
WEEKEND
GETAWAYS
OF TEXAS

INSPIRATION FOR THE MODERN-DAY EXPLORER

Jolie Berry

Published by

Signature
Boutique Books

www.signatureboutiquebooks.com

Publisher: Jolie Berry
Collaborating Partner: Brian G. Carabet
Associate Publishers: Kathy Shea, Andrea Simons, Courtney Williams
Editor: Katrina Autem
Graphic Designer: Shannon Catlett

Printed in the United States

Distributed by Independent Publishers Group
800.888.4741

PUBLISHER'S DATA

Spectacular Weekend Getaways of Texas

Library of Congress Control Number: 2017915010

ISBN 13: 978-0-9964240-3-5
ISBN 10: 0-9964240-3-2

First Printing 2018

10 9 8 7 6 5 4 3 2 1

This Page Top: Hotel Ella by Jake Holt
This Page Middle: Hotel Ella by Jake Holt
This Page Bottom: Hotel Ella by Jake Holt
Facing Page: Hotel Ella by Jake Holt
Previous Page: Stone House Vineyards image courtesy of Stone House Vineyards
Front Cover Image: Rancho Pillow by Knoxy Knox of Knox Photographics

WEEKEND
GETAWAYS
OF TEXAS

INTRODUCTION

My goal in publishing this book was to promote Texans to stay and play in Texas. I hope everyone who thumbs through these dazzling pages decides to take more road trips and make more memories discovering Texas. Admittedly, I have a love for Texas that runs deep. I'm a proud member of the Daughters of the Republic of Texas. I was born and raised in New Braunfels, where the Guadalupe and Comal Rivers were my playgrounds. My family took frequent weekend road trips to Port Aransas. I went to camp in the beautiful Hill Country of Comfort every summer. I got to explore West Texas during college and the big city of Dallas where I moved after college. I've traveled a lot, but some of the most memorable vacations were the ones I took right here in Texas to Rough Creek Lodge and the old Barton Creek Resort & Spa. There is so much to see and do in Texas, I knew this was a must-do book topic to publish. So here it is: *Spectacular Weekend Getaways of Texas*. And just in case you were wondering, it took me about a year to put this book together. I want to give a special thank you to my team who helped me along the way: Kathy, Courtney, Katrina, Shannon, Andrea, and to Brian Carabet, who has always been supportive and continues to be my trusted collaborator and partner in publishing. I hope you enjoy this pictorial journey through the Lone Star State's most exciting and noteworthy properties. Each chapter highlights the region's finest inns, hotels, resorts, B & Bs, and unique rental properties. Finding the authentic and the intimate is the holy grail for most of you travel-savvy folks. Thus, the featured properties are a curated collection that will allow you to make the most of your adventures and to uncover the delights of travel in Texas. Everything you see on the following pages was thoughtfully chosen. You will be introduced to a selection of outstanding overnight experiences that offer the Texas hospitality you expect. From the Hill Country to the city, there is something for everyone in this book. Whether you are looking for a romantic getaway, a healthy spa escape, or a fun family trip—this book is the perfect travel guide. The content of the book is separated into 5 chapters, making it easy for you to navigate and explore weekend escapes in your neck of the woods. Within each chapter are informative spotlight pages which feature a variety of amazing Texas towns and their most sought-after food, fun, events, entertainment, and fashion. So wherever your feet land, you'll have the perfect nearby restaurant or gallery to pursue. It's time for a road trip y'all!

Cheers,

Jolie

Fulton Harbor. Photograph by Marie Nesbit.

CONTENTS

*Sunset from Big Hill just South
of Alpine by Adam Holmes.*

TEXAS MAIN STREET PROGRAM

Texas is full of small towns with big personalities, and sometimes, if you don't pay attention it's easy to miss them. Each of these small towns have a story to tell, and everyone is just as history-filled and compelling as the next. Texas Main Street Program wants to promote small-town travel by inspiring communities to put life back into their districts and remind folks of the significance these places have in Texas history. Following a national lead on this rejuvenation trend, Texas now has 89 official Main Street Communities across the Lone Star State.

There's no reason to leave Texas when all of the shopping, dining, galleries, events, festivals, and historical sites are just a road trip away—or maybe even in your hometown. You can get a handheld travel guide by visiting texastimetravel.com. Download the mobile app and gain access to photos, videos, maps, visitor info, and mobile tours of places all across the state. It's a one-stop resource for trip planning, event searching, and historical information. You'll find all the cool festivals and learn facts that you never knew about the Lone Star State. Explore Texas and fall in love with the state all over again.

Photographs by Patrick Hughey.

Denton

Linden

Denison

Nacogdoches    Marshall

TEXAS HERITAGE
travel guide

There is no better state for road trips than Texas, and we're not just saying that because we're partial. Vast, beautiful, and full of hidden gems, the Lone Star State is ripe with getaway possibilities and travel opportunities. The hardest part of planning your escape is deciding where to go: lakes, mountains, beaches, cities, plains, historical sites, or event destinations. There are inns, restaurants, galleries, and trails in every nook and cranny of this great state.

To help you navigate it all, Texas Time Travel is an adventure-planning resource that you can take anywhere. The statewide travel guides are available for download, via mobile app, and some maps can even be ordered in print. Check in for up-to-date info on driving tours and upcoming events; think of it as a personal concierge service for all things Texas.

Explore by region or theme and find out where all of Texas' historical and cultural treasures are. If you'd like a road trip focused on Texas' military past for instance, then the Independence Region is your spot. Or maybe you'd prefer a seaside escape with plenty of fine dining? Head to the Tropical Region. There's even a Texas Historic Courthouse Preservation Program that highlights the state's most significant—and beautiful—county buildings. Whatever you're imagining, Texas Time Travel has your journey mapped out and ready to go. All you need is a long weekend, a travel buddy, and a full tank of gas.

Learn more about the historical sites of Texas at texastimetravel.com.

Photographs by Patrick Hughey.

Eisenhower Birthplace

Harrison County Courthouse

Starr Family Home

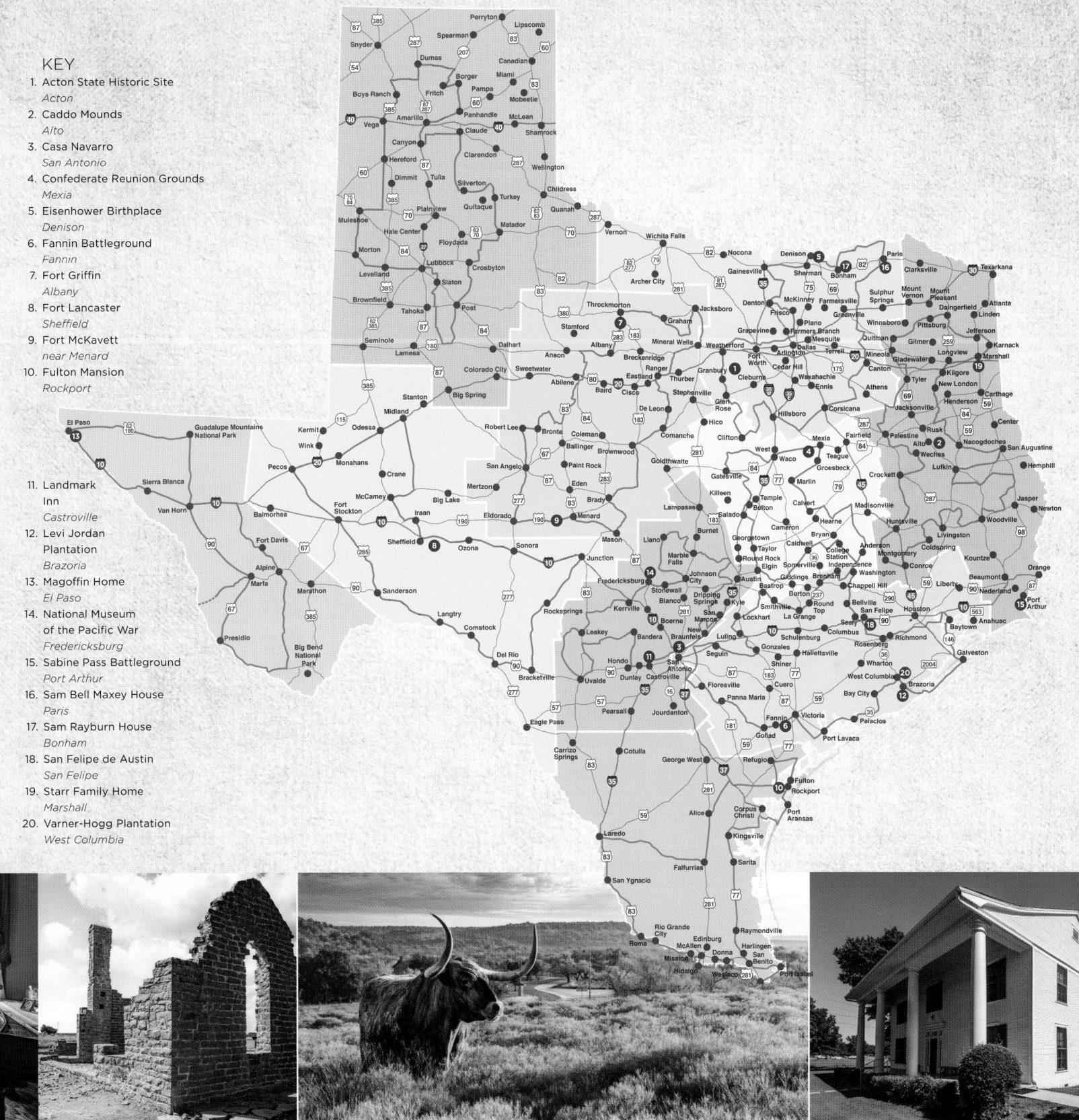

KEY

1. Acton State Historic Site
   Acton
2. Caddo Mounds
   Alto
3. Casa Navarro
   San Antonio
4. Confederate Reunion Grounds
   Mexia
5. Eisenhower Birthplace
   Denison
6. Fannin Battleground
   Fannin
7. Fort Griffin
   Albany
8. Fort Lancaster
   Sheffield
9. Fort McKavett
   near Menard
10. Fulton Mansion
    Rockport
11. Landmark Inn
    Castroville
12. Levi Jordan Plantation
    Brazoria
13. Magoffin Home
    El Paso
14. National Museum of the Pacific War
    Fredericksburg
15. Sabine Pass Battleground
    Port Arthur
16. Sam Bell Maxey House
    Paris
17. Sam Rayburn House
    Bonham
18. San Felipe de Austin
    San Felipe
19. Starr Family Home
    Marshall
20. Varner-Hogg Plantation
    West Columbia

Fort Griffin

Fort Griffin

Sam Rayburn House

Northern Region

Dinner is served at Los Pinos Ranch Vineyards
Photograph by Lori Ivey.

The Grove entrance in Tyler
Photograph by Tino Jaromillo.

View from Lush Resort on Possum Kingdom Lake
Photograph by Ryan Polk.

Wind turbines at 4R Ranch Vineyards

Photograph by John Sutton.

Sample Road Trip
Start: Dallas
End: Nocona
Miles: 107

Check into the groovy **Belmont Hotel** which boasts the best views of Downtown Dallas from the bar patio. The surrounding hip neighborhood has a plethora of chef-owned restaurants sure to please anyone's palate. For a relaxed dinner in one of Dallas' oldest and most popular cozy date night spots, try **The Grape Restaurant**. Need a night cap and some more action? You can go to **Javier's** cigar bar for head-turning people watching and stiff margaritas. Wake up and head to **Toulouse** for brunch. Think eggs Benedict, orange French toast, salad Nicoise, and beignets. Before leaving town, be sure to stop into the **Gypsy Wagon** boutique catering to the "footloose and fancy free." Head down Highway 30 West towards Fort Worth if you want to lay your eyes on the home stadiums for the Dallas Cowboys and Texas Rangers. Spend the afternoon in Fort Worth's world-class arts district. You can grab a snack at **Café Modern** inside the **Modern Art Museum**—everything is locally grown, fresh, and sustainable. If you are in the mood for shopping, be sure to stop in **Domain XCIV** for beautiful candles, antiques, dinnerware, accessories, and furniture.

Slow your roll as you approach the sweet town of Nocona where you can't miss the **Horton Classic Car Museum**. You'll find more than 40 Corvettes and other American vintage, classic, and muscle cars. Make your way over to **4R Ranch Vineyards and Winery** in Muenster for a glass of wine on the patio while taking in the most magnificent views of North Texas' Red River Valley. Be sure and check into Muenster's most popular events: Germanfest, Oktoberfest, and Nocona's **Vicari car auction**.

HIGH HILL FARM

—

*a boutique retreat tucked along
the rolling hills of East Texas*

Truly a one-of-a-kind retreat experience, High Hill Farm is a scenic 90-minute drive from Dallas through the rolling foothills of East Texas and just minutes from the historic town of Tyler. Combining laid-back luxury with the natural beauty of the region, High Hill Farm is the perfect getaway for guests looking to experience the good life, along with a variety of outdoor activities. Explore the retreat's 70 acres along winding paths through a forest of ancient oak trees, or relax by the sparkling reflection pool with stunning views of the vineyard. Enjoy casual dining with a farm-fresh twist at Côte, serving a seasonal menu of simple yet flavorful dishes. Then retreat to your private bungalow nestled along the picturesque hillside.

Featuring seven bungalows and a barn suite that sleeps up to six guests, High Hill Farm was featured by *Texas Monthly* in Where to Stay Now. The magazine also named High Hill's pool as one of the state's top 10 hotel pools. With simple yet elegant furnishings, luxurious linens, and oversize bathrooms with spacious walk-in showers, the accommodations are designed to impress even the most seasoned travelers. Each bungalow has its own private garden patio, making it the perfect place to relax, unwind, or enjoy al fresco dining. Escape to the country and discover why life is better at High Hill Farm.

Photograph by Ryan Polk.

12626 Country Road 217, Arp, TX 75750
214.929.6492 highhillfarm.com

Photographs by Amy Lu Photography (top, panoramic); Yvette Leihgeber (bottom left and right).

Photographs by Erica Mae Photography (bottom left); and courtesy of High Hill Farm (bottom right).

BELMONT HOTEL

—

boutique hotel near downtown with vintage appeal

There are more than a few things to love at the Belmont Hotel: the smell of barbecue, drinks at the bar, stargazing poolside, live music in the lounge, a chill evening in. The hotel features casual rooms and suites, vintage architecture, and minimalist design for travelers looking to disconnect—not disengage. Built in 1946, the hotel offers 64 rooms and suites that feature an understated style with modern amenities like free WiFi, a flat screen TV, and premier Lather bath products. Pet-friendly rooms are also available.

From a quick, quiet escape to a full vacation getaway, the Belmont Hotel is a great place to soak in the relaxing vibe and engage with other like-minded wanderers. A stay here means a visit to the core of Oak Cliff's burgeoning art and live music scene. Catch the newest up-and-coming artists hone their craft at one of the several nearby venues like The Kessler. View the latest exhibit or art installation at the Bishop Arts Theater Center. Or get nostalgic for the good old days and catch a movie at The Texas Theater. Occasionally The Belmont will host live music, so be sure to check their calendar regularly.

Photographs courtesy of the Belmont Hotel.

901 Fort Worth Avenue, Dallas, TX 75208
866.870.8010 belmontdallas.com

spotlight
DALLAS
HIGHLAND PARK VILLAGE

Nestled in one of Dallas' most stunning neighborhoods, Highland Park Village is the go-to spot for truly exceptional shopping and dining experiences in a historic, Spanish-inspired setting. A variety of contemporary and luxe brands line charming walkways including alice + olivia, Beretta Gallery, Cartier, CHANEL, Fendi, Hermes, Jimmy Choo, custom boot maker Miron Crosby, rag & bone, Theory, Veronica Beard, and more. Guests can enjoy everything from beauty and atelier boutiques, fine jewelry, personalized gifting and children's fashion, as well as movies at the legendary Village Theatre built in 1935.

Restaurants in Highland Park Village offer a virtual trip around the world with global flavors at some of the city's most stylish culinary destinations, ranging from casual to elegant. Dine at Bistro 31, Café Pacific, FACHINI, The Honor Bar, Mi Cocina, and Perfect Union Pizza Co. for classic staples with locally sourced ingredients, or stop by and savor a sidewalk café at Bird Bakery or Royal Blue Grocery, an upscale urban market and coffee shop.

HIGHLAND PARK VILLAGE
Highland Park Village, Dallas, Texas 75205
214.443.9898 hpvillage.com

Photographs by Laura Wilson (left and center) and Peter A. Calvin (right).

THE HONOR BAR

26A Highland Park Village, Dallas, Texas 75205
214.780.0956 honorbar.com/locations/dallas/

Photograph by Manny Rodriguez.

MIRON CROSBY

225 Highland Park Village, Suite 201, Dallas, TX 75205
214.238.3385 mironcrosby.com

Photograph by Chandler Mann.

spotlight
DENISON

Denison's "moving forward, kicking back" attitude sums up the unique spirit of this beautiful North Texas city. Downtown is a designated historical district, an entertainment district, and an arts and cultural district. Events happen almost weekly and include live music, festivals, and parades. Visitors can stroll along Main Street to experience "small town big art" and tour art destinations including Mary Karam's Art Gallery, Sparrows Gallery, and 413 Maker's. Denison is one of the few Texas cities to feature multiple craft beverage venues including Homestead Winery, Ivanhoe Ale Brewery, and Ironroot Republic Distillery.

Visitors should check out the Eisenhower Birthplace State Historical site, the 1890-birthplace of the 34th president, Dwight D. Eisenhower. The visitor center celebrates Ike with memorabilia and exhibits highlighting his service as president and as a war hero. Nearby Lake Texoma boasts plenty of recreational opportunities such as largemouth bass fishing, water sports, and dinner cruises. Visitors can campout under the stars at Eisenhower State Park or enjoy popular marina services of nearby Grandpappy Marina, Eisenhower Marina & Yacht Club, Highport Marina, and Tanglewood Resort. Don't miss the scenic drive across the iconic Denison Dam and the historic Carpenter's Bluff Bridge over the Red River. For more information, check out denisontexas.us.

Eisenhower Birthplace

Ironroot Republic Distillery

Grandpappy Point Marina Compass Rose Ship

Mary Karam Gallery

DENISON VISITORS CENTER

313 W. Woodard, Denison, TX 75020

903.465.1551 denisontexas.us

Photograph by Mel Climer.

IRONROOT REPUBLIC DISTILLERY

3111 Loy Lake Road, Denison, TX 75020

903.337.0495 ironrootrepublic.com

Photograph by Cristi Brinkman.

GRANDPAPPY POINT MARINA

132 Grandpappy Drive, Denison, TX 75020

903.465.6330 grandpappy.com

Photograph by Mel Climer.

MARY KARAM GALLERY

404 W. Main Street, Denison, TX 75020

903.465.3703 marykaramgallery.com

Photograph by Mary Karam.

WINDING RIDGE
BED & BREAKFAST

—

country sophistication just outside of Dallas

If you could create a place that captured all the charm and beauty of Texas, it would be Winding Ridge Bed & Breakfast. It is located on 22 rolling acres outside of Ennis, just 30 minutes south of Dallas on one of the city's official bluebonnet trails. Guests can take advantage of premium star gazing, beautiful sunrises and sunsets on the wrap-around porch, or cozy up to the rock fire pit.

Looking for a bit of the peaceful farm life? Winding Ridge lets guests interact with their onsite animals—meet the donkeys, goats, and horses. Stroll through the scenic countryside. With plenty of nearby backroads, the lodging has become a favorite among biking enthusiasts and motorcyclists.

Accommodations have a refined rustic feel, with a leather couch, vintage claw-foot tubs, and primitive antiques. Enjoy the refreshing stonewashed Belgian linens from Restoration Hardware and the plush robes provided for your pampering. Relax on the covered patio or in front of the wood burning fireplace. Continental breakfast items are provided, including the farm's fresh eggs. Winding Ridge is an ideal romantic getaway, as well as a retreat for intimate weddings, reunions, and family stay-cations. It's so peaceful, you'll forget you're near a big city.

Photograph by Parrish Ruiz De Velasco.

512 Sugar Ridge Road, Ennis, TX 75119
214.543.3057 windingridgebb.com

Photographs by Michaella Ramler (opposite page), Shaun Meanary Photography (this page, top), Parrish Ruiz De Velasco (this page, bottom left and right).

spotlight
ENNIS

As the Official Bluebonnet City and Trail of Texas, Ennis is the best place to see the rolling fields of Texas' most beautiful flower. The Ennis Bluebonnet Trails Festival is a springtime celebration that welcomes thousands of visitors to see the blooms and enjoy live music, wine tasting, food sampling, children's activities, and so much more.

THE ENNIS BLUEBONNET TRAILS FESTIVAL

200 NW Main Street, Ennis, TX 75119
972.878.4748   bluebonnettrail.org

Photograph by Ashley Colunga.

See what Ennis is all about in historic downtown. Shop, stroll, eat, and relax in the heart of the city. The brick streets and vintage storefronts give the area an Old World charm that has defined Ennis' character. Tuesday through Saturday are the best days to make your shopping trek downtown.

HISTORIC DOWNTOWN ENNIS

200 NW Main Street, Ennis, TX 75119
972.878.4748   visitennis.org

Photograph by Jina Armstrong Photography.

Help Ennis embrace its Czech heritage and celebrate all things polka at the National Polka Festival; it kicks off with a parade through historic downtown every Memorial Day weekend. There will be polka music, traditional costumes, Czech food, and dancing, of course. This festival is fun, quirky, and full of personality.

NATIONAL POLKA FESTIVAL

200 NW Main Street, Ennis, TX 75119
972.878.4748 nationalpolkafestival.com

Photograph by Jim Martin.

THE TEXAS WHITE HOUSE

—

urban art-clad boutique bed & breakfast

Ask proprietor Cindy Lucio what her secret to running a winning bed & breakfast is and she'll tell you, "We simply focus on the bed and the breakfast." Cindy and her small team run The Texas White House Bed & Breakfast with a strong emphasis on the accommodations, or the bed, if you will. Rooms have every modern amenity a guest could need, from comfortable bedding and artistic décor, to the locally made soaps and bath salts with essential oils. The breakfast is equally important at her establishment. Guests are served an artfully plated, chef-prepared menu with the farm-to-table concept.

The Texas White House Bed & Breakfast sits within walking distance from the heart of Magnolia Avenue in the Near Southside area of Fort Worth. The bed & breakfast is great for small events, as the Texas Star Garden plays host to weddings and dinner parties of 50 people or less. If you're an art lover, you're in for a real treat: the bed & breakfast doubles as an art gallery that promotes local artists. Every year, Cindy and husband, Javier, hold two open houses to showcase new artists and a few guest rooms, too. Local guests, as well as others from around the world, view and often purchase art pieces during their stay.

Photographs by Mariajose Cervantes (bottom left) and Leo Wesson (all others).

1417 8th Avenue, Fort Worth, TX 76104
817-923-3597 texaswhitehouse.com

30

ROUGH CREEK LODGE AND RESORT

—

world-class resort with five-star dining and a Texas edge

Is it possible for a place to have a soul? Can a location have a personality? If you've ever visited Rough Creek Lodge and Resort, you'll say the answer is yes, and it's taken 20 years to develop. Rough Creek is a Texas-style resort that caters to everything you could want: chef-driven dining, luxury spa, hunting, horseback riding, fishing, climbing wall, zip line, swimming pools, and enough activities to occupy kids—and adults— for an entire season. The resort is also a popular choice for weddings and corporate outings.

Rough Creek Lodge has an unmistakable warmth, and that comes directly from the 100-plus member team that has a sincerity that cannot be mistaken. The food is sensational and fresh, and comes from a very talented chef. Every menu is made from scratch—breakfast, lunch, and dinner. But what keeps the guests coming back season after season? The service. Rough Creek has an exclusive-club feel with luxury service that's hard to come by, and it's made guests fall in love with the resort.

And that's not all. Rough Creek just announced a new and exciting ownership opportunity: The Residences at Rough Creek Lodge. It's an exclusive community of two and three-plus bedroom homes that offer spacious floorplans with modern and sophisticated furnishings that reimagine Rough Creek Lodge's signature charm and service. Visit liveroughcreek.com.

Photograph courtesy of Rough Creek Lodge.

5165 Country Road 2013, Glen Rose, TX 76043
800.864.4705 254.965.3700 roughcreek.com

Photographs courtesy of Rough Creek Lodge.

Photographs on this page and opposite page by Bernardo Medina, courtesy of Rough Creek Lodge.

spotlight
GLEN ROSE

If natural history and outdoor adventures are your speed, Glen Rose is your next destination. As the Dinosaur Capital of Texas, the town has Dinosaur Valley State Park and Dinosaur World. Both offer cool dinosaur adventures like examining foot prints, seeing life-size, animatronic dinosaurs, and going on fossil hunts. The Creation Evidence Museum also has dinosaur prints, plus a 25-foot replica of Noah's Ark, artifacts from Native American Indians and Israel, a biosphere, petrified wood, and so much more.

Still looking for more outdoor adventures? Fossil Rim Wildlife Center gives visitors a savannah experience. You can feed the giraffes, see endangered species, or enjoy a guided mountain bike trail. Visitors can also play in the Paluxy River at Big Rocks Parks for water adventures. If you prefer something a bit more refined, have no fear. Glen Rose has plenty of those activities, too. Take a stroll down the River Walk to the historical downtown square for shopping and dining, head to the Somervell County Expo Center for shows and events, or explore the Squaw Valley golf course. Like festivals? The Lone Star State Dulcimer Championship and Festival is held in Glen Rose, along with two annual three-day bluegrass music festivals—Glen Rose is also the bluegrass Capital of Texas, after all. For more information, check out glenrosetexas.org.

BIG ROCKS PARK

NE Barnard Street, Glen Rose, Texas 76043
254.897.3081 glenrosetexas.net

Photographs courtesy of Glen Rose CVB.

COURTHOUSE SQUARE

NE Barnard Street, Glen Rose, Texas 76043
254.897.3081 glenrosetexas.net

CREATION EVIDENCE MUSEUM

3102 FM 205, Glen Rose, Texas 76043
254.897.3200 creationevidence.org

FOSSIL RIM
WILDLIFE CENTER

2299 County Road 2008, Glen Rose, Texas 76043
254.897.2960 fossilrim.org

LUSH RESORT

—

new upscale resort on Possum Kingdom Lake

With lush rolling hills, towering limestone cliffs, and deep, clear water, Possum Kingdom Lake is the perfect escape from the concrete jungle—just two hours west of Dallas.

While honeymooning in the Abacos, Bahamas, owners Bo and G Bennett were inspired to bring a bit of the island life home to Texas. During the last three years, the couple has been transforming the old iconic Scuba Point into the new, coastal-modern Lush Resort.

Guests enjoy an island feel while lounging in the pool listening to Reggae, sipping piña coladas, and watching kids play on the beach. WaterRush, located on the Lush beach, ensures that guests get a fun-filled lake experience with boat rentals, paddleboards, kayaks, and exhilarating Jetovator Flights.

Accommodations include six one-bedroom suites, twenty full hook-up RV sites and a three-bedroom home. Each 600-square-foot suite has a fresh, beach-house feel with large porches overlooking the lake, spacious living areas with fully equipped kitchens, comfortable Simmons Beautyrest king beds separated by privacy doors, and luxurious bathrooms. Whether you are staying on-site or just popping in for lunch, all guests enjoy the Lush Life.

Photographs by Johnny Latham.

3201 Redbird Road, Graford, TX 76449
940.779.3731 possumkingdomlushresort.com

INN ON LAKE GRANBURY

—

luxury lodging on the lake

Thinking of a getaway for a special occasion or just to relax? The award-winning Inn on Lake Granbury, located less than 90 minutes from Dallas and 45 minutes from Fort Worth, is an upscale lakefront inn and retreat in historic Granbury. The inn offers luxury accommodations for exceptional romantic getaways, beautifully orchestrated weddings, and a relaxing venue for group retreats. The town has wonderful restaurant choices, art galleries, live theater, and great shopping. Experience wineries too, just a short drive from the inn.

As a testament to its popularity, Inn on Lake Granbury is honored to be in the exclusive Select Registry, the industry's most upscale small lodging association. And it's no wonder why—this getaway has it all. Imagine a romantic walk down winding pathways to the lake's edge or perhaps relaxing by the pool or on the bluff beneath live oak trees overlooking the lake. Experience oversize two-person jetted tubs, fireplaces, sweeping balcony views, or soothing body jets and steam sauna units in showers— all while enjoying your stay wrapped in the finest bed linens and the comfort of luxurious robes. A full breakfast is also included, plus complimentary wine and appetizers in the late afternoon. If you are looking for rest and relaxation, the Inn on Lake Granbury is the place to be.

Photographs by Jumping Rocks Photography.

205 West Doyle Street, Granbury, TX 76048
817.573.0046 innonlakegranbury.com

spotlight
GRANBURY

Long known for celebrating its past, Granbury is now more focused on the present. The historic town square, the first in Texas to be named to the National Register of Historic Places, is filled with shops, galleries, and restaurants that wouldn't be out of place in bigger cities, such as Dallas or Fort Worth. But unlike its urban neighbors to the north, Granbury's streets are traffic-free and the stars shine brightly overhead. Stress is seldom seen and most visitors leave feeling energized.

What you find in Granbury are amazing meals, scenic views, and seemingly endless activities to keep your family entertained. There are restaurants for every taste, plus a nearby brewery, and three local wineries. There's even an artisanal cheesemaker to complement your Cabernets and Chardonnays before you lead your family on an extraordinary adventure. Local events range from the renowned Granbury Wine Walk in April and the Harvest Moon Festival of the Arts in October, to eclectic and family friendly gatherings. For nature lovers, Lake Granbury offers hours of fun, including boating, fishing, and water sports. Plan your getaway today at visitgranbury.com.

Photographs courtesy of Visit Granbury Inc.

Enjoy picturesque historical architecture

Town square is on the National Register of Historic Places

Lake Granbury offers tons of activities for visitors

Sip samples from three local wineries

Fun, eclectic boutique shops abound

spotlight
GRAPEVINE

Unforgettable experiences await in Grapevine. Located 25 minutes from Dallas or Fort Worth, Grapevine boasts authentic Texas charm and offers something for every traveler. With a full range of accommodations for any budget, Grapevine is home to luxurious options such as the Gaylord Texan Resort on Lake Grapevine, as well as national hotel favorites.

Historic Downtown Grapevine features more than 80 locally owned shops, boutiques, galleries, restaurants, and more. Sip and savor award-winning wines along Texas' premier Urban Wine & Craft Brew Trail, containing 10 tasting rooms, two craft breweries, and a cidery.

Grapevine is home to world-class festivals and events throughout the year, such as SummerBlast; Christmas Capital of Texas®, featuring 1,400 events in 40 days; Main Street Fest – A Craft Brew Experience; and GrapeFest®, the largest wine festival in the Southwest.

Step aboard the Grapevine Vintage Railroad's authentic 1920s-era Victorian coaches and enjoy excursions along the historic Cotton Belt Route. Guests can also take the Grapevine Visitors Shuttle to top-tier restaurants and live entertainment venues. Learn more at grapevinetexasusa.com.

Grapevine welcomes millions of visitors annually

Photographs courtesy of the Grapevine Convention & Visitors Bureau.

Discover delicious Texas wines along the Urban Wine Trail

Guests enjoy dinner under the big Texas sky at Nash Farm

Journey back in time aboard the Grapevine Vintage Railroad

Crushing grapes during GrapeStomp at GrapeFest®

HOUSE OF
THE SEASONS

—

*Victorian escape with
all the elegant details*

Built in 1872, House of the Seasons has as many stories to tell as you'd expect a century-and-a-half-old home would have. The beautiful Victorian has hosted the likes of American presidents and first ladies—George Bush and Lady Bird Johnson—and country music legends and authors, such as Lyle Lovett and Pat Conroy. The home's interior features Greek Revival and Victorian elements, most notably the large cupola and murals. Inside the cupola, each wall features a work of colored stained glass that gives the illusion of the four seasons. Guests will also appreciate the home's impressive art collection and authentic period pieces from the 19th century.

Now owned by the Calvert K. Collins Family Foundation, House of the Seasons has four elegant suites to choose from, each with its own personality and character. The Epperson Suite features a king-size bed with luxury linens, lush robes, and a private bath. Romantic and refined, the Presidential Suite offers a two-person Jacuzzi, an antique writing desk, and a cozy Victorian sitting area. Visitors will feel relaxed and taken care of, whether visiting for a wedding, escaping for an anniversary weekend, or traveling for work. House of the Seasons accommodates any special occasion.

Photographs by Heavenly Reflections by Sam Ayer.

409 South Alley Street, Jefferson, TX 75657
903.665.8000 houseoftheseasons.com

TWIN OAKS PLANTATION BED & BREAKFAST

—

historic home in the Piney Woods

With details reminiscent of the Parthenon, this stately Southern Colonial Greek Revival home is located on a historic 1813 Spanish land grant. It's nestled between the Big Cypress and Little Cypress Rivers next to one of Jefferson's earliest roads. The six-acre grounds were originally part of a cotton plantation that later became a pecan plantation—typical crops for the area during that time. The present owners, Mr. and Mrs. Alan Yarbrough of Mansfield, Louisiana, purchased the land in 2010 for family and future gener-ations. The property has since been extensively renovated by Joe McDonnell of McDonnell Construction. He and his wife Carmen manage the operation and are the innkeepers for Twin Oaks Plantation Bed & Breakfast.

The homes on the property are filled with intricate architecture, custom molding, and woodwork styles that reflect a passion for antiquity. Twin Oaks, as well as the 1873 antebellum cottage and pool house, are filled with exquisite antiques from around the world, many of which date back to the 1800s. The getaway is an ideal setting for a girls' weekend, anniversary, or a backdrop to host your special event.

Photograph by Terri Eddington of Legacy Photography LLC.

2620 FM 134, Jefferson, TX 75657
903.665.3535 twinoaksjefferson.com

TEXAS FOREST COUNTRY RETREAT

—

luxurious getaway nestled in the ruins of a historic Texas town

Imagine that you are driving down an old country road with dense forest on all sides, thinking that you may be lost, and all of a sudden an opening in the woods appears. In the middle of nowhere you see a large old white house overlooking a lake. Then your curiosity is assuaged by a historical marker that explains that you have found the site of the old, turn-of-the-century sawmill town of Manning, Texas. You discover that there was a damaging fire on January 3, 1935, and all that remains is the timber baron's mansion, the sawmill lake, and some concrete and brick ruins.

You are really excited to see that the old mansion has been turned into a bed & breakfast and there is a vacancy just for you. Of course, you check in and you are immediately confronted with beautiful architecture and vintage furnishings replete with an incredible history of a bygone era.

This old Mansion on Sawmill Lake offers guests a trip back in time but with all the conveniences and amenities of today. It boasts of red brick columns, large front and back porches with rocking chairs, two balconies, a library, and four beautiful guestrooms. This was once the childhood home of the owner Bob Flournoy, an attorney and businessman who lives nearby. You can get all the details at texasforestcountryretreat.com.

Photographs by MSGPR.

156 Grimes Flournoy Road, Huntington, TX 75949
936.639.4466 texasforestcountryretreat.com

MANSION
ON
SAWMILL
LAKE
JESUS IS

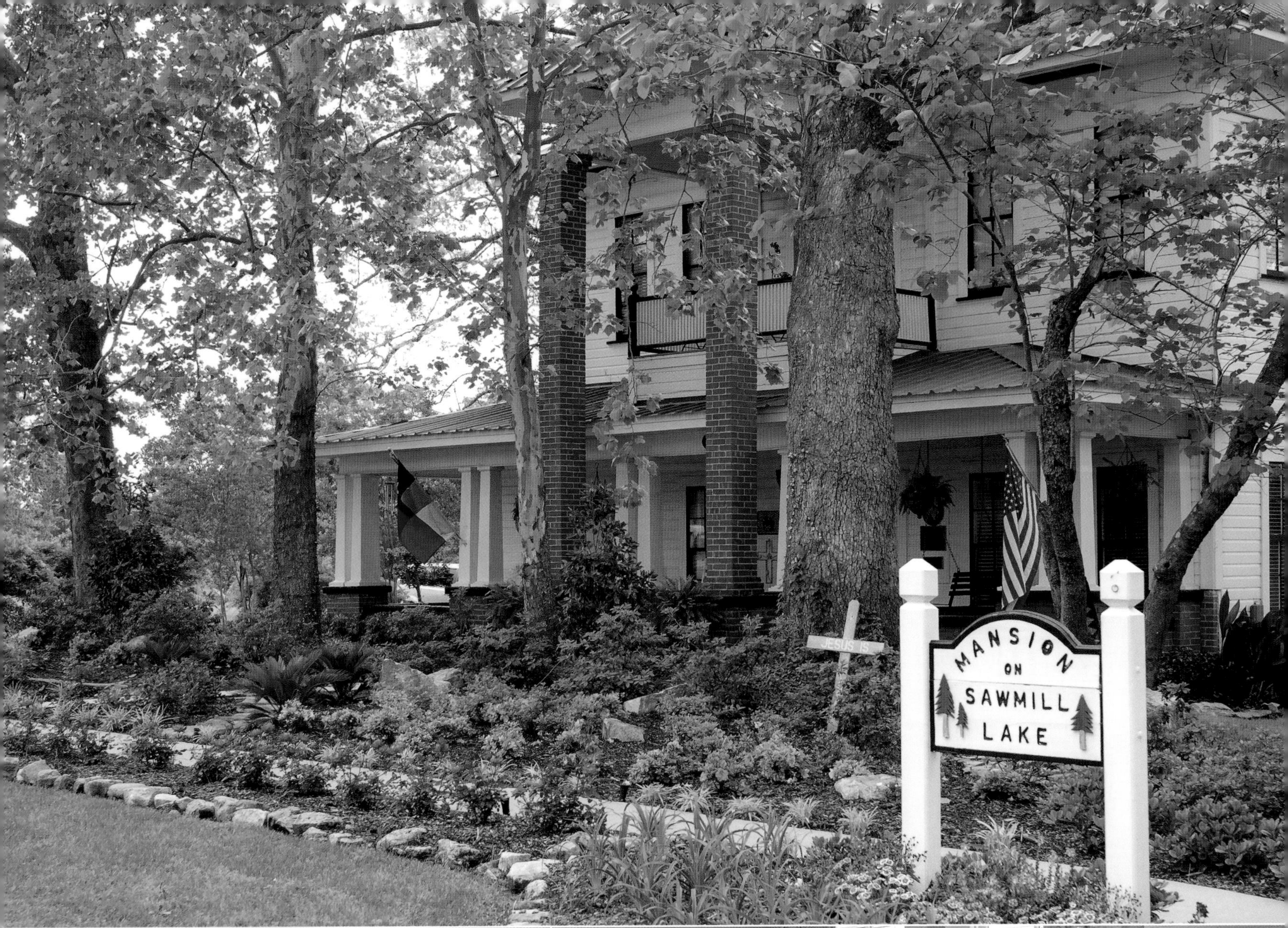

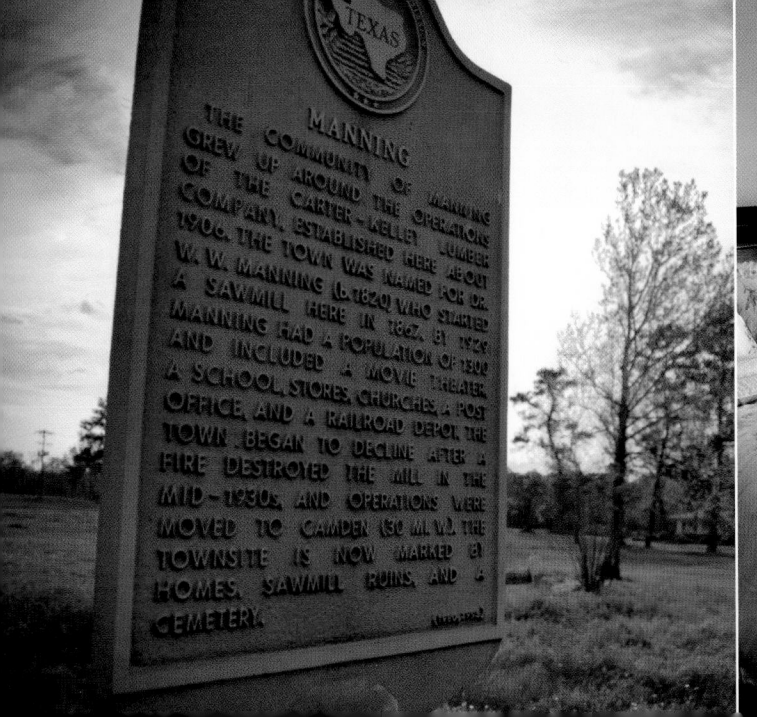

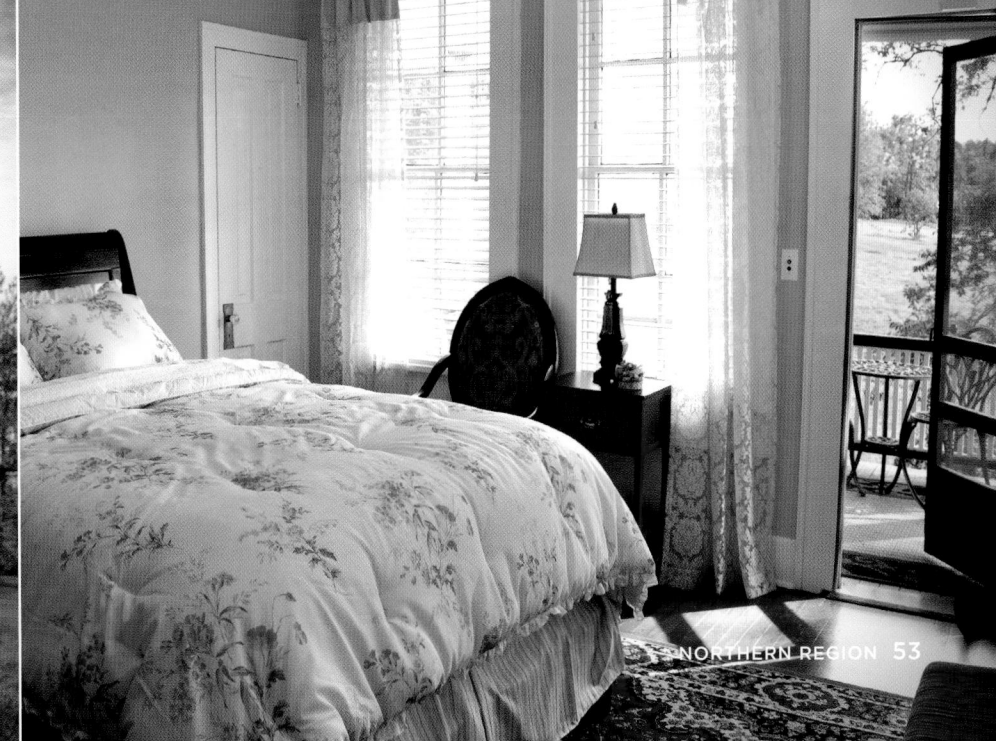

TEXAS
MANNING
THE COMMUNITY OF MANNING
GREW UP AROUND THE OPERATIONS
OF THE CARTER-KELLEY LUMBER
COMPANY, ESTABLISHED HERE ABOUT
1906. THE TOWN WAS NAMED FOR DR.
W. W. MANNING (B. 1820) WHO STARTED
A SAWMILL HERE IN 1867. BY 1929
MANNING HAD A POPULATION OF 1300
AND INCLUDED A MOVIE THEATER,
A SCHOOL, STORES, CHURCHES, A POST
OFFICE, AND A RAILROAD DEPOT. THE
TOWN BEGAN TO DECLINE AFTER A
FIRE DESTROYED THE MILL IN THE
MID-1930s, AND OPERATIONS WERE
MOVED TO CAMDEN (30 MI. W.). THE
TOWNSITE IS NOW MARKED BY
HOMES, SAWMILL RUINS, AND A
CEMETERY.

4R RANCH VINEYARDS & WINERY

—

great wines with the best views in the North Texas hill country

Where the shortgrass prairie drops into the Red River Valley, the 4R Ranch—with its magnificent vistas and rocky terrain—is perfectly suited for growing grapes. Patriarch W.C. Roper encouraged his family of sixth-generation Texans to share the beauty of this extraordinary place with others; and so it was love of this man and love of the land that inspired 4R Ranch Vineyards & Winery. Powered by sun, earth, and wind, 4R Ranch Vineyards & Winery calls visitors to slow their pace, enjoy the view, and sip a glass of wine in the magnificent Red River Valley.

The Wind Shed Tasting Room, which takes its name from the strong breezes that power the wind turbines on the property, is the perfect place to relax, unwind, and enjoy 4R wines. The tasting menu features estate wines produced from the viognier and cabernet sauvignon vineyards on the ranch, as well as a collection of white, rosé, and red wines produced from carefully sourced grapes to please many palates.

At the entrance to the ranch is a small house, ideal for weekend rentals and families of brides and grooms. The three-bedroom home features a full kitchen, living room and an outdoor sitting area with an herb garden where guests can relax and take in the views of the vineyards and Camp Creek.

Photographs by John Sutton Photography.

1473 County Road 477, Muenster, TX 76252
940.736.3370 4Rwines.com

THE FREDONIA HOTEL
AND CONFERENCE CENTER
—
*an authentic boutique experience
in Nacogdoches*

Located in historic downtown Nacogdoches less than a mile from Stephen F. Austin State University, The Fredonia Hotel was established and built by the town citizens in 1954. The people sold stock in order to raise funds to build the now legendary hotel. After changing hands several times, The Fredonia was purchased by Richard and Barbara DeWitt in 2014 in an effort to rejuvenate and rebuild a piece of the town's history. After more than $15 million in investments and two years of restoration, the hotel came back to life, with all of its architectural beauty, history, and memories intact. All rooms and public spaces have been renovated, as well as the pools.

The Fredonia has a café that serves breakfast, lunch, and dinner with an eclectic menu that appeals to all kinds of tastes and personalities, plus a steakhouse with world-class cuisine. There is also a bar called 9 Flags, a favorite spot for locals and travelers alike. Other amenities include a high-end, boutique-style gift shop, a 24-hour gym, and an inviting terrace space for lounging by the pool and watching the large-screen TV.

Photographs by Wendy Floyd.

200 N. Fredonia St., Nacogdoches, TX 75961
936.371.1190 thefredonia.com

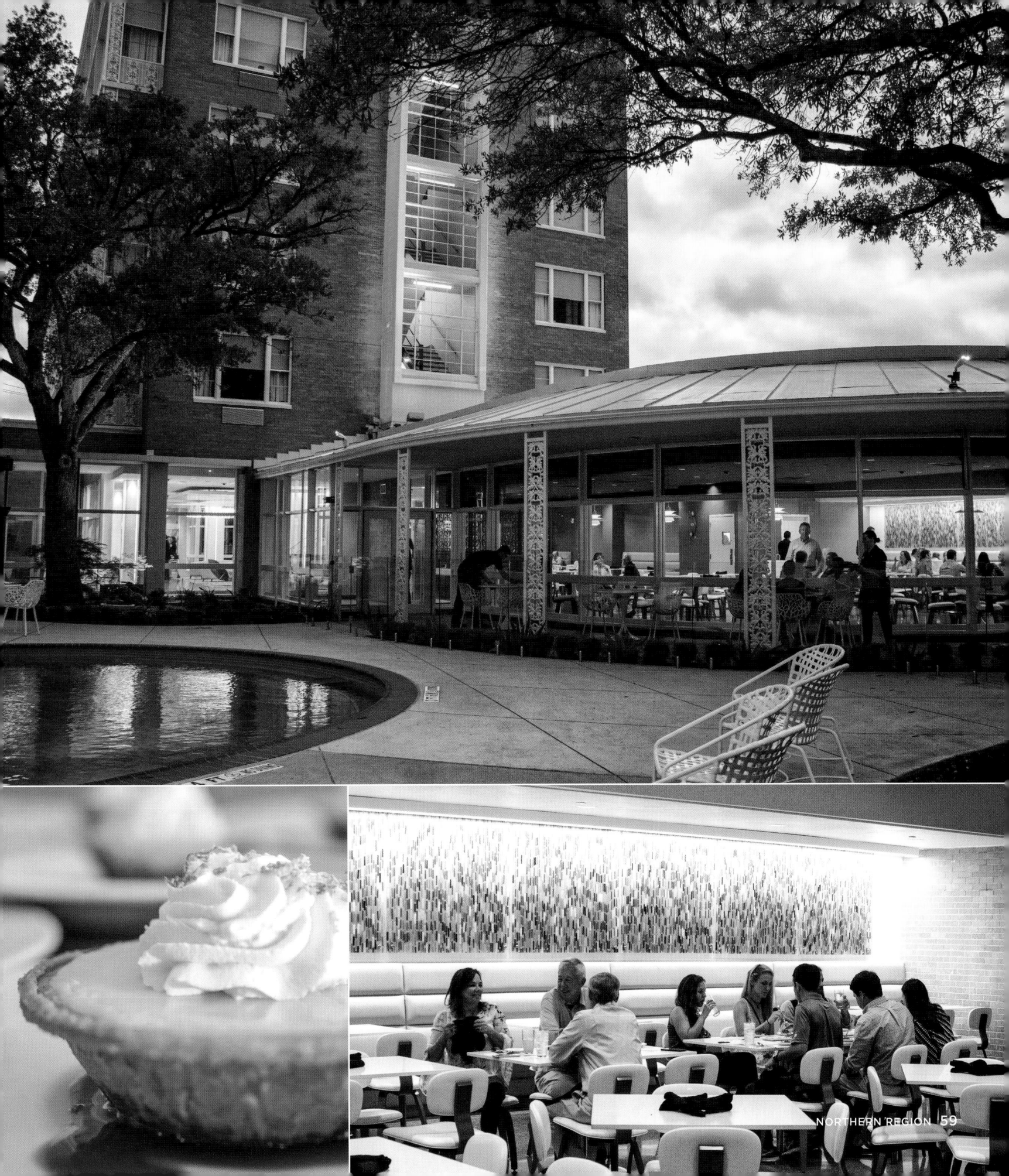

spotlight
NACOGDOCHES

Welcome to Nacogdoches. As one of the top 10 tourist destinations in Texas, the city offers some of the best live music and entertainment. Visitors and locals alike frequent The Liberty Bell Bar—a hub of young Southern talent that brings music lovers from all over the state. There are also plenty of great restaurants, boutique shopping, and hotels that rival big-city accommodations. Known for its variety of libations, Naca Valley Vineyard is a favorite spot, along with the downtown Fredonia Brewery, and Front Porch Distillery. Looking for something that involves a little more nature? Nacogdoches—the Garden Capital of Texas—is proud of its dozen-plus public gardens, including the beautiful Ruby M. Mize Azalea Garden.

THE LIBERTY BELL
422 East Main Street, Nacogdoches, TX 75961
936.622.6425 libertybellbar.com

Photograph courtesy of Nacogdoches CVB.

NACA VALLEY VINEYARD
9897 FM 1878, Nacogdoches, TX 75961
936.615.6432 nacavalley.com

Photograph by Greg Patterson.

As the "oldest town in Texas," the city is no stranger to historical charm. The story of Nacogdoches includes Caddo Indians, Spanish settlers, the Mexican government, and famous Texans like Stephen F. Austin—namesake of the well-known university. With tons of historical landmarks and museums to tour, Nacogdoches is clearly proud of its storied past. Old Nacogdoches University Building is a favorite with visitors; the one-time Confederate hospital was built in 1859 and remains as the only structure from a once-bustling university. Don't be fooled by the deep history and brick-laid streets, though. This town knows how to party. For more information, check out visitnacogdoches.org.

RUBY M. MIZE AZALEA GARDEN

2107 N. University Drive, Nacogdoches, TX 75961

936.468.3301 visitnacogdoches.org

Photograph courtesy of Nacogdoches CVB.

OLD NACOGDOCHES UNIVERSITY BUILDING

515 N. Mound Street, Nacogdoches, TX 75961

936.569.7292 olduniversitybuilding.com

Photograph courtesy of Nacogdoches CVB.

spotlight
NOCONA

Love cars? Then you'll want to check this out. From its headquarters in Harvey, Louisiana, Vicari Auction Company conducts classic and muscle car auctions all across the South, including venues in Nocona, New Orleans, and Biloxi. Pete Vicari's passion for American muscle cars, specifically Corvettes, inspired him to enter the Classic & Muscle Car Auction Arena in Biloxi more than 20 years ago. His pastime hobby has grown into a successful auction business that attracts hundreds of cars to each event—sales reach into the millions of dollars. Pretty cool, huh? Learn more at vicariauction.com/nocona-tx.

VICARI CAR AUCTION
210 West Walnut Street, Nocona, TX 76255
504.264.2277 vicariauction.com/nocona-tx

Photograph courtesy of Vicari Auction.

The Horton Classic Car Museum is housed in what once was the town's Ford dealership. More than 138 cars are contained in the collection in 37,400 square feet of space. Largely focused on American vintage, classic, and muscle cars, the museum has more than 40 Corvettes as part of the collection, featuring nearly every year of production between 1953 and 1978. Several 1950s-era convertibles are also included, along with many 1950s Senior Award winners from the Chevy and Pontiac Nationals. Different models of Chevrolets, Fords, Pontiacs, Packards, Plymouths, Oldsmobiles, and even a Studebaker, are featured in the collection which is always changing and growing. See for yourself at hortonclassiccarmuesum.com.

HORTON CLASSIC CAR MUSEUM

115 West Walnut Street, Nocona, TX 76255

940.825.1022 hortonclassiccarmuseum.com

Photographs by Shadow Ridge Graphics.

THE REDLANDS HISTORIC INN

—

East Texas elegance on Main Street

Specializing in extended stays, The Redlands Historic Inn offers visitors ideal East Texas lodging. The inn has reduced rates for monthly and weekly guests but gladly takes nightly patrons on short notice. People from all over the country use the inn as a temporary home while exploring the region's vast geography and rich history. The area was once a booming center for oil, lumber, cattle, and cotton, surrounded by major railroad lines—the towns all have stories to tell.

Set in the middle of Palestine's historic district, the inn is close to bars, restaurants, and a bustling main street. The building itself reveals the town's past, as it was once an elegant, state-of-the-art Edwardian structure. With no shortage of character, the brick, concrete, and metal building still dons original doors, tilework, wood trim, stair railing, and plaster finishes. But don't be fooled by the vintage details—no modern convenience is spared. Every room is equipped with contemporary upgrades, vibrant colors, updated styles, and lightning-speed Wi-Fi. The Redlands Inn is a welcoming link between the region's past and travelers' needs of today.

Photographs by Dave Shultz Commercial Photography.

400 North Queen Street, Palestine, TX 75801
903.729.2345 redlandshistoricinn.com

spotlight
PALESTINE

If you're trying to choose a place for your next getaway in the Lone Star State, make sure that Palestine is on your short list. Named by *Texas Highways Magazine* as a Top 40 Travel Destination, Palestine has historical sites, arts and cultural events, architectural gems, festivals, outdoor fun, and nightlife—all with loads of East Texas charm.

Perhaps the town is best known for its blooming dogwoods in spring, or that it is home to the official railroad of Texas, the Texas State Railroad, but there are plenty of other attractions that will spark your attention. Love history? Check out the Museum for East Texas Culture: a 1915 schoolhouse with an authentic period classroom, log cabin, and railroad artifacts. Architecture buffs should be sure to check out the Howard House Museum which showcases the quintessential Greek Revival style, the beaux-art Anderson County Courthouse, the Carnegie Library, one of 13 remaining in Texas, and the North and Southside Historic Districts full of architecture dating back to the 1850s. Food lovers and fun seekers will feel right at home here too, with local events like the Hot Pepper Festival, Palestine Main Street Wine Swirl, Neches Wilderness Canoe Race, the Polar Express Train Ride, and so many more.

Photographs courtesy of the Texas State Railroad (top left), courtesy of Visit Palestine (top center), by Stuart Whitaker (top right), and by Dave Shultz (bottom left and right).

Home to the Texas State Railroad

Plenty of entertainment and night life

Springtime brings blooming dogwoods

Tour the Museum for East Texas Culture

Parts of Palestine will feel like a nostalgic step back in time

LOS PINOS RANCH VINEYARDS

—

a destination winery with a serious culinary twist

Los Pinos Ranch Vineyards is nestled deep within the Piney Woods of East Texas just south of Pittsburg. It offers food and wine enthusiasts a respite from the chaos of everyday life. The winery is a relaxing oasis where everyone is welcome, offering wines from the estate vineyards and Texas High Plains vineyards. Its nationally acclaimed restaurant with tasting room serves up wine varietals and blends that pair perfectly with tapas, wood-fired cuisine, and chef specials served at this rustic setting overlooking the vines. There's also plenty of live music with no cover charges and no reservations needed.

Owned by native Texans, Los Pinos is operated under the notion that it's important to enjoy life and to always have fun. Impressive and uncomplicated, the international award-winning wine list boasts true Texas terroir. There's something for every palate at all levels. The team is happy to answer questions while educating guests; no pretentiousness found here. Tuscan cottages are available for couples seeking a bit of escapism, wine, and romance, or for those looking for an event space, the ranch also serves as a beautiful venue for weddings, celebrations, and corporate gatherings. It's truly a little hidden gem where the secret's out.

Photographs by Lori Ivey Photography.

658 County Road 1334, Pittsburg, TX 75686
903.855.1769 lospinosranchvineyards.com

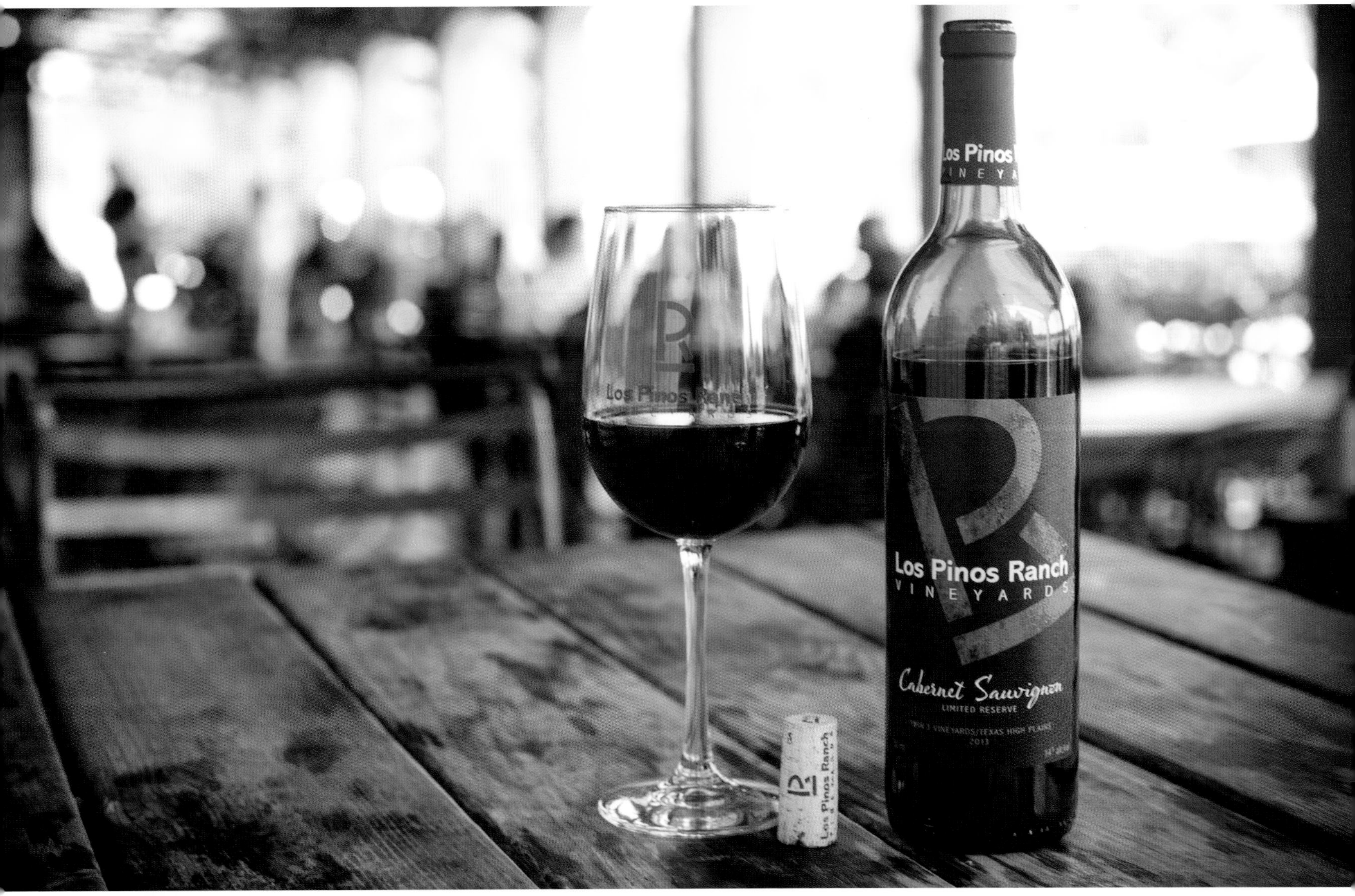
Los Pinos Ranch
VINEYARDS
Cabernet Sauvignon
LIMITED RESERVE
2013

Los Pinos Ranch
VINEYARDS
Vermentino
Rosato
Sangiovese
Meritage

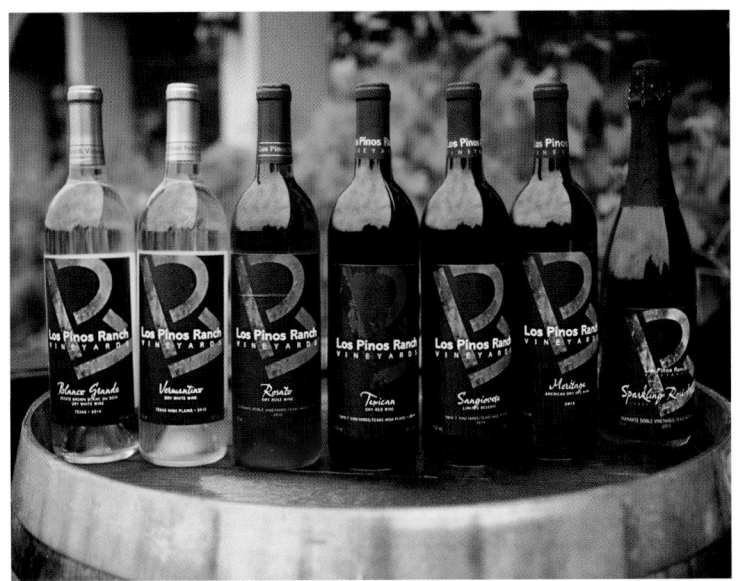

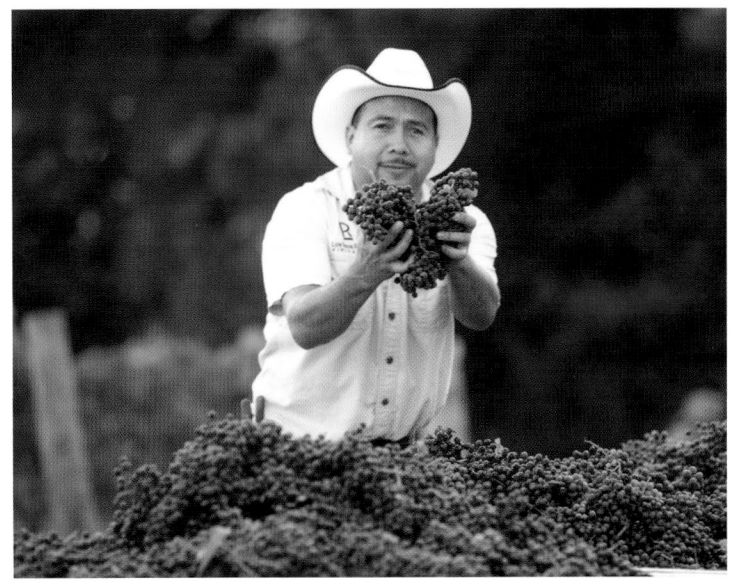

TANGLEWOOD RESORT

—

fun-filled resort on Lake Texoma

Tanglewood Resort couldn't be situated in a better location. Just next to Highport Marina on a small cove tucked away on Lake Texoma, the resort sits peacefully in the North Texas town of Pottsboro. The lake offers top-notch boating, fishing, beaches, and tons of water activities—but the resort offers so much more. There's basketball, tennis, volleyball, horseshoes, a three-tiered waterfall swimming pool, an indoor fitness center, horseback riding, an outdoor Jacuzzi, and nearby hiking. Golfers are in for a special treat, as they can enjoy the private 18-hole course designed by Arnold Palmer and architect, Ralph Plummer. The lush, 7,000-yard Bermuda fairway is suitable for a range of skill levels. Want something a little more relaxing? There's a full spa to really enjoy your escape and take your mind off of reality.

If you're looking for a conference space or banquet hall, Tanglewood has you covered. They're known for their business accommodations, as well as reception space for weddings, reunions, team-building retreats, and more.

The iconic eight-story tower features six suites and a lounge, and was designed and built by the great mid-century architect O'Neil Ford. From there, Tanglewood expanded to a resort with 120 rooms and a conference center. The villas are as large as 1,500 square feet and have full kitchens, private bedrooms, and walk-in closets. You may never want to leave.

Photographs courtesy of Tanglewood Resort.

290 Tanglewood Circle, Pottsboro, TX 75076
844.424.1030 tanglewoodresort.com

spotlight
TYLER

One visit to Tyler and you'll see why this Texas town is considered a natural beauty. The Rose Capital of America, Tyler is home to the largest municipal rose garden in America, with more than 500 varieties of the flower on 14 lush acres. The entire month of October is dedicated to the rose, with festivals and celebrations for the whole family to enjoy. The Azalea & Spring Flower Trail is a springtime celebration that takes visitors on a 10-mile stretch through residential gardens and historic home sites—and it's stunning. Tyler State Park, Goodman-LeGrand House and Museum, and Kiepersol Winery also offer some of the most beautiful scenery in the South.

Art and history museums are big attractions in Tyler, with options like the Gallery Main Street, Historic Aviation Memorial Museum, Liberty Hall, Brookshire's World of Wildlife Museum, and the American Freedom Museum. There are also notable performing and fine arts venues to check out, including a nationally recognized art museum.

All this exploring making you hungry? You're in luck. Tyler has some of the most memorable restaurants in the state with a variety of cuisines: The Grove, Kiepersol, Bernard Mediterranean, Stanley's Famous Pit Bar-B-Q, and Dakotas, to name a few. Plan your getaway at visittyler.com.

Goodman-LeGrand House and Museum

Gallery Main Street

Stanley's Famous Pit Bar-B-Q

The Grove

GOODMAN-LEGRAND HOUSE AND MUSEUM

624 N Broadway Ave, Tyler, TX 75702

903.531.1286 parksandrec.cityoftyler.org

Photograph courtesy of Visit Tyler.

GALLERY MAIN STREET

110 West Erwin St., Tyler, Tx, 75702

903.593.6905 downtowntylerarts.com

Photograph by Kevin Young, Aperture 42 Photography.

STANLEY'S FAMOUS PIT BAR-B-Q

525 S Beckham Ave, Tyler, TX 75702

903.593.0311 stanleysfamous.com

Photograph courtesy of Visit Tyler.

THE GROVE

3500 Old Jacksonville Highway, Tyler, TX 75701

903.939.0209 thegrovetyler.com

Photograph by Tino Jaramillo.

spotlight
WICHITA FALLS

What if you could have everything the big city offers with all of the small-town comforts? It may seem too good to be true, but it does exist, and it's probably much closer than you think. Located between Dallas-Ft. Worth and Oklahoma City, Wichita Falls offers the best of both worlds. Leave behind the urban hustle. It's all about local here, and that's all you need.

Family friendly and full of Southern charm, Wichita Falls has something for just about everyone. Art, music and theatre lovers will be especially impressed with the city's strong artistic culture. Foodies can enjoy top Texas steakhouses and barbeque, as well as cafes and bakeries with artisan appeal. Wichita Falls is also home to Midwestern State University, the state's only public liberal arts college. Each year, MSU hosts hundreds of events that are open to the public, leaving a broad impact on the region.

If you're still not convinced Wichita Falls should be the destination for your next road trip, consider this: there's no traffic. That's something city dwellers will forever appreciate. Local attractions are easily accessible and traveling around town is low stress. Perhaps the most telling trait of Wichita Falls, however, is the friendliness of its residents. You definitely won't feel like a stranger when you visit, and you may never want to leave.

Iron Horse Pub

The Karat

River Bend Nature Center

Wichita Theatre

IRON HORSE PUB

615 8th Street, Wichita Falls, TX 76301
940.767.9488 theironhorsepub.com

Photograph by Jeanette Charos.

THE KARAT A GANACHE CO.

800 Ohio, Wichita Falls, TX 76301
940.766.3000 ganacheco.com

Photograph courtesy of Wichita Falls Convention and Visitors Bureau.

RIVER BEND NATURE CENTER

2200 3rd Street, Wichita Falls, TX 76301
940.767.0843 riverbendnaturecenter.org

Photograph by Samantha Abeyta.

WICHITA THEATRE

925 Indiana Avenue, Wichita Falls, TX 76301
940.723.9037 wichitatheatre.com

Photograph courtesy of Choose Wichita Falls.

CLARK HOUSE BED & BREAKFAST

—

sophisticated East Texas getaway

Wouldn't the ideal bed & breakfast provide all of the comforts of home but have none of the responsibilities? The Clark family and staff achieve this at Clark House Bed & Breakfast with detail-oriented service and warm, welcoming accommodations. The Clark property encompasses three unique facilities to include the original carriage house, a beautifully renovated century-old home, and a 3,000-square-foot event center that sit in Winnsboro, also affectionately called the Austin of East Texas. As a Texas Designated Cultural Arts District, the small town has big personality. Art shows, live music, acclaimed restaurants, farmers markets, car shows, and high-end boutiques and salon make this town worth visiting—and revisiting. Dining options include steakhouses, new American, and South African cuisine that can compete with any big city fare. Looking for something a little more outdoorsy? Many nearby lakes, including Lake Cypress Springs, offer top-notch fishing, boating, hunting, and kayaking for adventurous types.

Regarded as the nicest accommodations in town, the Clark House Bed & Breakfast consists of large, comfortable rooms with private bathrooms. Guests are welcome for extended stays and can enjoy the colorful gardens, sitting areas, stone porches, and outdoor fireplaces. If visitors are planning a special occasion getaway, the Clark House can customize a weekend package—think fishing and hunting trips, girls' weekend, or a pampered spa stay, even a wedding. The possibilities are endless.

Photographs by Blackard Media.

100 East Cedar Street, Winnsboro, TX 75494
903.588.0465 clarkhousewinnsboro.com

GREER FARM

—

a peaceful rest in the rural life

How often do you get to spend time on a real working farm? For most people, it's a rare treat to see the simple life, far away from the bustle of urban stress. Greer Farm offers this experience to visitors, with appealing accommodations on its nearly 400 scenic acres.

There are four log cabins and a two-bedroom barn loft for guests to choose from, all with access to a private, 11-acre, spring-fed lake. Paddle boats, canoes, kayaks, and paddleboards are available, along with ideal fishing. Visitors get a chance to gather eggs from the hen house, interact with baby farm animals, and pick fresh berries—an all-time favorite. During June and July, three varieties of blackberries and five types of blueberries are plentiful, sweet, and ready for guests to harvest and enjoy.

Purchased in 1979, the farm has been working since the 1840s and raised everything from sweet potatoes to watermelon to peanuts. Today, Sid, Eva and their small team run the farm on the principles of sustainable agriculture: conservation, preservation, animal welfare, and organic practices. The Texas Department of Agriculture aptly stated that the Greer Farm is the only one of its kind, and you'll probably agree.

Photographs courtesy of Greer Farm.

1444 County Road 1125, Daingerfield, TX 75638
903.645.3232 greerfarm.com

MOORE VENTURA BED AND BREAKFAST

—

a timeless small-town retreat

If you appreciate attention to detail and historical accuracy, Moore Ventura Bed and Breakfast is the ideal getaway. Capturing the essence of Southern charm, the home has been meticulously restored to show off the beauty of its original Neoclassical Revival design. The fluted doric columns and roofline balustrades have a story to tell—and guests love hearing it. Malinda Anderson and Captain Hardin T. Moore combined their respective fortunes in 1892 when the widowed pair wed, living on a ranch east of Ennis until their dream home was complete. Little did they know, the new home would eventually become a cornerstone of Ennis' architectural history and attract visitors from across the country.

The stunning house was purchased 17 years ago by owners and innkeepers Sam and Joanne Ventura, until they realized it was simply too beautiful to keep hidden. They now welcome every kind of traveler—from honeymooners to businessmen—with the most comfortable of accommodations and the tastiest of menus. Breakfasts are no small affair here; they're prepared fresh, daily, in-house. Served on pressed white linen tables and wedgewood plates, the gourmet meal can range from eggs Benedict to raspberry French toast. The chefs, Sam and Joanne themselves, even take special requests.

Photograph by Sam Ventura.

400 West Denton Street, Ennis, TX 75119
972.878.7300 mooreventurabedandbreakfast.com

THE FAIR BREEZE COTTAGE

—

peaceful haven for nature lovers

Looking for a quiet respite away from it all? Fair Breeze Cottage in Nacogdoches is the ideal getaway. Innkeepers Stan and Christie Cook aim to make every guest happy and feel right at home. The warm vintage style and welcoming décor inside the cottage, in addition to a spectacular view overlooking 46 acres of forest and meadow, provides guests a myriad of relaxing activities in a pastoral setting.

Guests can enjoy sinking into an outdoor screened-in hot tub while listening to the surrounding wildlife. Wake up at your leisure and enjoy cinnamon rolls and coffee while watching the sunrise from the front porch. For outdoor enthusiasts, extensive nature trails throughout the property are available for hiking, along with two ponds for fishing. Bird watchers find this getaway an absolute paradise, which includes Carolina wrens, cardinals, blue birds, white-eyed vireos, indigo buntings, and more. Feeling a little more adventurous? Check out the quaint and historic town of Nacogdoches, the oldest town in Texas. Visitors will delight in meandering through the brick streets that are lined with antique shops and quaint restaurants, along with the town's museums, cultural festivals, rodeos, art exhibitions, theatre productions, and more.

After visiting Fair Breeze, guests will find it hard to leave.

Photographs by David White (left, bottom right) and courtesy of Fair Breeze Cottage (top right).

4741 County Road 724, Nacogdoches, TX 75964
936.615.1150 fairbreezecottage.com

THEE HUBBELL HOUSE BED & BREAKFAST

—

wooded Southern dream

Want to take a step back in history? If you're looking to escape to simpler times, Thee Hubbell House is for you. The 1888 Southern Plantation-style home has been beautifully preserved, with period antiques and historic details. The large white columns, porches, balcony, and centuries-old oak trees welcome guests to this woodsy East Texas gem. The immaculate gardens provide a calming spot to stroll, relax, and enjoy the peaceful setting. Visitors can rest in the Amish swing, by the pond, gather around the fire pit, or at the in-ground salt water pool.

Owned and operated by Tim Carmichael, Thee Hubbell House has gained attention from a regional publication, awarded best bed & breakfast three times and placed in the magazine's hall of fame. Guests can choose from several accommodations in the Carriage House or the Mansion. Rooms offer varying amenities—claw-foot tub, garden views, private entrances, modern appliances, Wi-fi, and large flat screen TVs. The front and rear porch of the Mansion, and the second-story balcony, provide common areas for guests to sit and enjoy the grounds, a cup of coffee, or a glass of wine. A delicious full country-style breakfast will greet you in the Mansion dining room at your selected time.

Photograph by Tim Carmichael.

307 West Elm Street, Winnsboro, TX 75494
800-227-0639 theehubbellhouse.com

Central Region

Camp Comfort
Photograph courtesy of Camp Comfort.

Overlooking the River Walk at Hotel Valencia
Photograph by Jerry Hayes.

Juicy steak at Peggy's on the Green
Photograph by Jason Reisner.

San Saba sunset

Photograph by Mitch Hallmark.

Sample Road Trip
Start: Austin
End: Port Aransas
Miles: 252

Start your weekend getaway at **Hotel Ella**, conveniently located in the heart of Downtown Austin. You don't even have to leave the property for fine dining at the onsite restaurant **Goodall's**. If you must hit the town, you might want to try one of Austin's local favorites, **Guerro's Taco Bar,** for killer Tex Mex. If you're in the mood for something more elegant, try **Jefferey's** for dry aged beef and a stellar wine selection.

Wake up and hit highway 35 South and head to your first stop in San Marcos for the best ribs in the state at **The Tap Room** on the square in San Marcos. Keep trucking down 35 to Gruene—this charming riverside town is bustling on weekends. **Gruene Market Days** is a monthly event with dozens of artisans selling their goods. You'll want to stop into **The Grapevine** where you can explore a tasting of Texas wines. Walk across the street to **The Gristmill** for the best chicken-fried steak you'll ever taste! If you're not too stuffed, grab a root beer float or a Moonpie at the nostalgic **General Store**. Just steps away, check into your room at the **Gruene Mansion Inn** to rest up or hit **Gruene Hall** and two-step the night away.

On your way to Port Aransas, you'll want to peel off the highway for a peek at San Antonio's historic brewery complex **Pearl Brewery**, offering dining, shopping, a year-round farmers market and daily events. You'll find a very exciting food scene celebrating regional traditions inside this culinary destination. You can grab some fresh ingredients for a picnic on the beach when you arrive in Port A. Check into your house at the seaside community at **Cinnamon Shore** and enjoy the Texas beach.

NO DIVING

AUSTIN MOTEL

—

*classic motor court
with far-out interiors*

The Austin Motel opened its doors in 1938, and its landmark neon sign has been brightening South Congress Avenue ever since. The redesign was inspired by a few decades that stand out in the motel's history: the 1930s, when it was built; the 1950s, when it was in its heyday; and the 1980s, when Austin was at the end of its cosmic cowboy era, just before the city started changing. Operating under the mantra "So close. Yet so far out," this recently remodeled 41-room motel, with classic motor court exterior, is centrally located in the heart of Austin's most interesting cultural district and close to downtown. The 24-hour reception desk and retail store caters to guests' needs and offers snacks, drinks, and quirky mementos.

Photographs by Nick Simonite.

1220 South Congress Avenue, Austin, TX 78704
512.441.1157 austinmotel.com

HOTEL SAINT CECILIA

—

secluded rock and roll decadence

In late 2008, hotelier Liz Lambert opened the Hotel Saint Cecilia. Named in honor of the patron saint of music and poetry, the hotel takes cues from a 1960s image of the Rolling Stones lounging on the lawn of a distinguished estate—rock 'n' roll decadence overrunning uptight society. With only 14 rooms, the property offers seclusion and a high level of dedicated service. Every room has a turntable, vinyl library, antique and mid-century furniture, Turkish rugs, 1970s posters, art installations, and other unique elements. A small pool, an exclusive lounge, bungalows, and a taxidermied white peacock perched above the bar round out the impossibly creative offerings. Hotel Saint Cecilia is a 14-room luxury hotel situated on the grounds of an 1880 estate in the heart of Austin. Each of the five distinct suites, six poolside bungalows, and three studios set amidst the lush, wooded grounds have been designed to inspire the artist in each guest and offer a quiet escape from the world.

Photographs by Nick Simonite.

112 Academy Drive, Austin, TX 78704
512.852.2400 hotelsaintcecilia.com

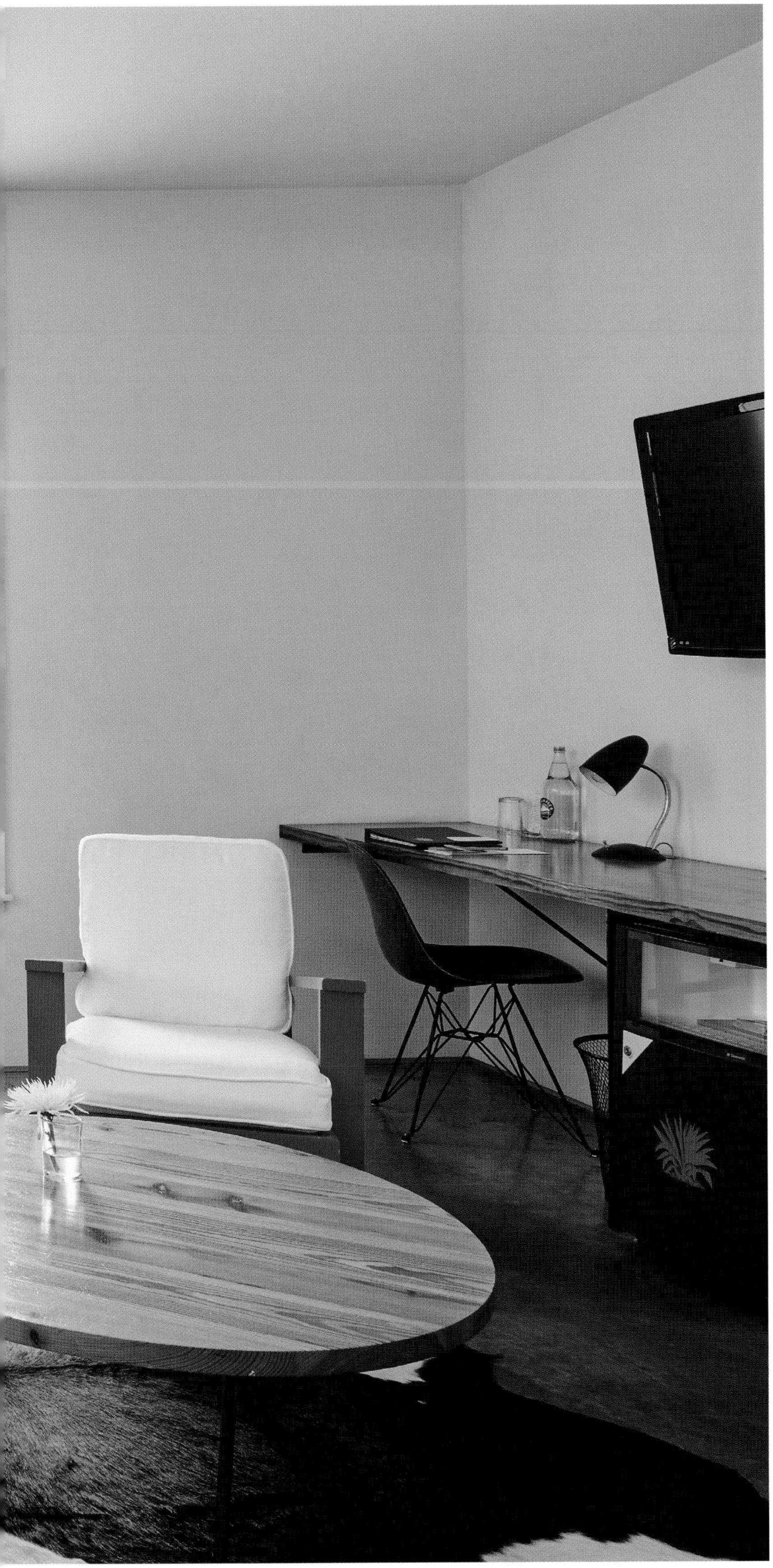

HOTEL SAN JOSÉ

—

minimalist, urban bungalow

Hotel San José was once an ultra-modern motor court and the place to stop on your way to San Antonio in the 1930s. By 1997, it had fallen into disrepair, until former prosecutor Liz Lambert came along and changed all that. She ran the hotel for three years to accrue funding, then commissioned Lake|Flato Architects to transform it into a 40-room Texas minimalist hotel in a garden-courtyard setting. The hotel is located along South Congress, amid cafés, boutiques, and the bustle of Austin's streets. Lush and green, the grounds are rich with succulents and other native and exotic plants. The soothing courtyard, inviting interiors, unique décor, custom-made sheets and bathrobes, and carefully curated mini bars, make Hotel San José a Texas favorite. It is also home to Jo's, a popular neighborhood coffee shop, meeting place, and people-watching outpost.

Photographs by Nick Simonite.

1316 South Congress Avenue, Austin, TX 78704
512.444.7322 sanjosehotel.com

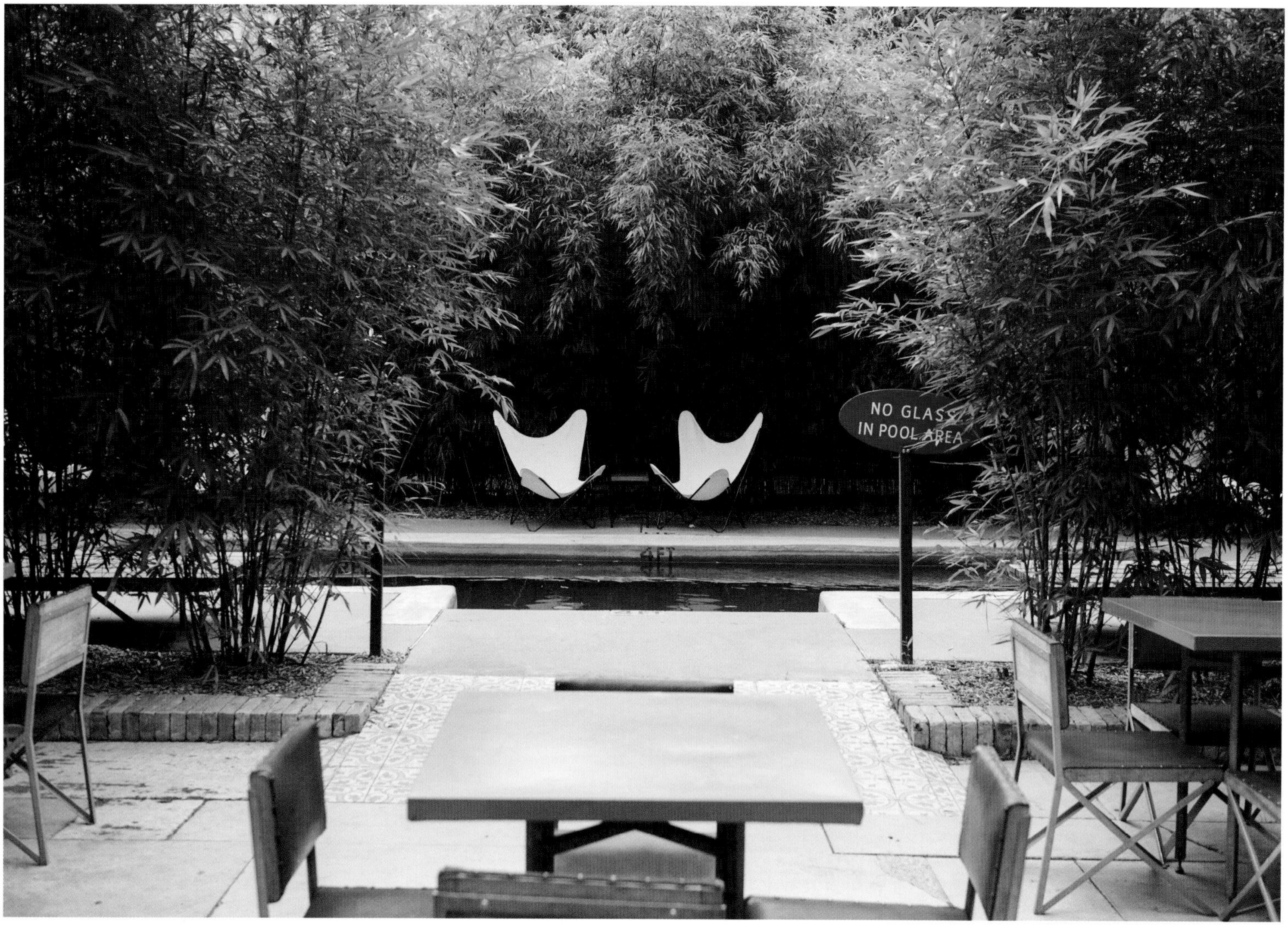
NO GLASS
IN POOL AREA

WELCOME
HOTEL
SAN JOSE

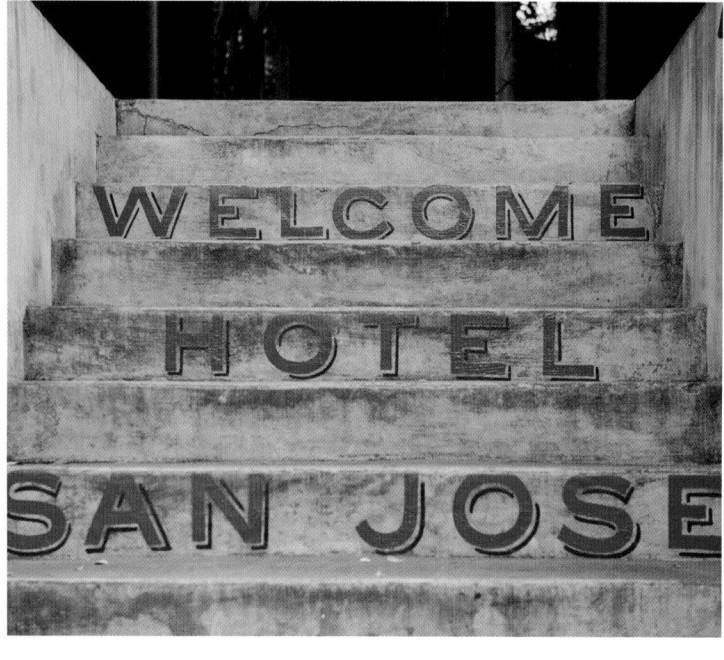

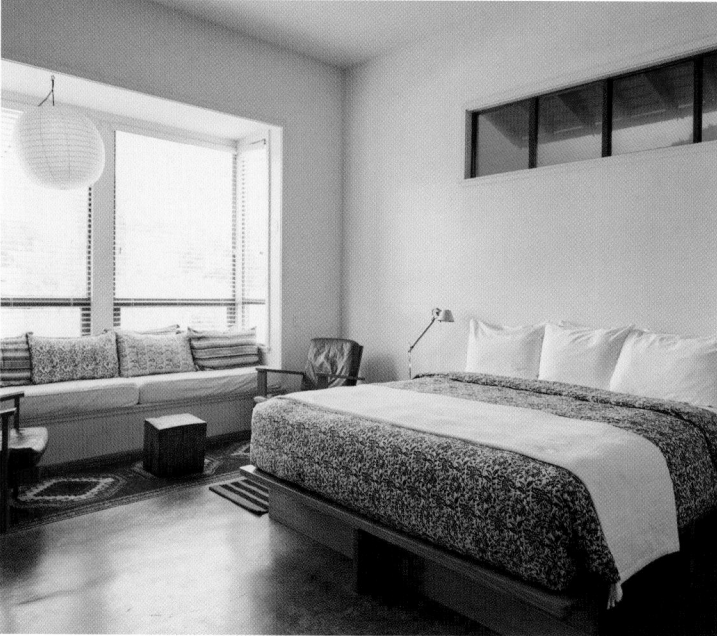

TAPATIO SPRINGS HILL COUNTRY RESORT

—

a true Texas original

"Come for a good time, stay for a long time," as owner and partner George Strait says. Nestled in the Hill Country, Tapatio Springs shows off warm welcomes, hard work, charming service, and Texas hospitality. The crew is proud to offer quality amenities, outstanding food, drinks, and experiences. Songwriters & Storytellers, a weekly live performance series, features top local and regional talent at the La Cascada Table & Bar on the weekends; and for a taste of Texas cuisine, the chef's brunch is not to be missed.

With $3.5 million in resort enhancements, including the golf course restoration and Double L Pool and Bar, Tapatio Resort is on every event planner's short list. The newly completed meeting renovation has transformed the resort's event spaces into some of the best venues in Texas Hill Country. Just 35 minutes northwest of San Antonio, Tapatio Springs is an ideal setting for relaxation, respite, and reconnection. Beyond business, the resort offers memorable team-building experiences, many in partnership with Enchanted Springs Ranch. The resort doesn't skimp on the things that matter, because the only thing that makes the team happier than meeting new friends is seeing old ones return. Kick up your boots and enjoy.

Photographs courtesy of Tapatio Springs Hill Country Resort.

1 Resort Way, Boerne, TX 78006
830.537.4612 tapatioresort.com

Nestled in the scenic Hill Country, Boerne is located just north of San Antonio and southwest of Austin. The town features activities for any occasion, including romantic getaways, student trips, girls' weekends, bachelor escapes, or family vacations. There are plenty of outdoor adventures—visitors love the Cibolo Nature Center and Guadalupe River State Park—and city-lover activities such as shopping, dining, and musical events. Restaurants include everything from fine dining to barbecue. If you love it, you'll find it in Boerne.

Guests will love the historically elegant building with a bakery and bistro serving breakfast, lunch, and dinner. The boutique features home accents, apparel and gifts, a bookstore, and a custom-designed event venue.

THE DIENGER TRADING CO.

210 North Main Street, Boerne, TX 78006
830.331.2225 thediengertradingco.com

Photograph by Snap Chic Photography.

Cibolo Creek Brewing Co. is a family-owned brew pub featuring unique farm-to-table fare and an assortment of creative craft brews.

CIBOLO CREEK BREWING CO.

448 Main Street, Boerne, TX 78006
830.816.5275 cibolocreekbrewing.com

Photograph by JoMando Cruz.

More than just a mile, the Hill Country Mile is a walkable stretch of unique shopping, dining, art, festivities, and outdoor adventure right through the historic heart of downtown Boerne.

HILL COUNTRY MILE

Downtown Boerne, Boerne, TX 78006

hillcountrymile.com

Photograph by West Vita.

Casual yet elegant, this Southern-inspired restaurant and craft-cocktail bar was created by the chef and owner of nationally renowned Bohanan's Prime Steaks and Seafood. It has remained a local favorite for years.

PEGGY'S ON THE GREEN

128 West Blanco Road, Boerne, TX 78006

830.572.5000 peggysonthegreen.com

Photograph by Jason Reisner Photography.

MYSTIC QUARRY

—

seek a higher campground

Whether you're a first-rate glamper or you love the idea of roughing it, Mystic Quarry is a campsite resort that caters to everyone's style. Set in the Hill Country, the campground offers a range of accommodations to suit your preferences, such as tiny houses and dog-friendly cottages with modern comforts and an urban-living feel. Campers can also opt for a 22-foot diameter, Sioux-style tipi—yes, a real tipi with HDTV, air conditioning, comfy beds, and cowhide furnishings. Have your own RV? No problem. Drop anchor under the oak tree groves that wind through the grounds and stay awhile. And of course, for the camping purists, the site also offers ideal spots for primitive camping under the starry skies. No worries, though. You still have access to laundry facilities and a bath house, plus plenty of other cool amenities.

The large meeting hall, pool, shady arbors, hammocks, rooftop deck, nature trails, and lawn games make Mystic Quarry an ideal location and setting for corporate outings and family reunions. You can use Mystic Quarry as your basecamp to visit nearby towns and the best tubing river in Texas, the Guadalupe River. Also catch the seasonal Friday night series Music Under the Stars, featuring local artist entertainment in the courtyard.

Photographs by Peter Bardenhagen (aerial photo, opposite), Jim Trent (this page, center and bottom). All other photographs by Trey Daffin.

13190 FM 306, Canyon Lake, TX 78133
830.964.3330 mysticquarry.com

ONION CREEK KITCHENS AT JUNIPER HILLS FARM

—

ultimate foodie retreat

Some places manage to strike the perfect balance of what you really want. With just the right amount of fun, food, and relaxation, Onion Creek Kitchens at Juniper Hills Farm is an ideal getaway for foodies. The retreat offers guests specialized culinary classes suited to any level of cook. Titles like *Soups and Bread*, *Three Easy Fishes*, and *I Love Cupcakes* give food lovers a chance to enjoy the experience of cooking from a trained instructor. Not in the mood to cook? Onion Creek Kitchens also offers "spectator" spots for those who enjoy food without getting their hands dirty. The light-filled, spacious venue is the perfect spot for your next private party or celebration.

Started by Sibby Barrett, the retreat has comfortable cabins for visitors, set against the peaceful backdrop of the Hill Country's creeks and vistas. Lodging includes beautiful amenities like hand-painted Mexican sinks and mirrors, luxury linens, private rock patios, and sunrise views. Plus, guests can pick their favorite forms of relaxation and fun—yoga classes, saunas, an infinity pool, bocce ball courts, or fire pits. The rooms also include a stocked, rotating bookshelf for those who just want to curl up with a good book. There really is no wrong way to relax here.

Photographs by J. Noel Photography.

5818 Ranch Road 165, Dripping Springs, TX 78620
830.833.0910 juniperhillsfarm.com

COTTON GIN VILLAGE AND CABERNET GRILL

—

rustically romantic cabin lodging for foodies

Romantic. Historic. Memorable. For a Texas getaway unlike any other, head to Cotton Gin Village in Fredericksburg and see why people love this bed & breakfast. Not quite your ordinary lodgings, the accommodations are made up of seven rustic cabins that take you back to a simpler time. Guests get to experience the authenticity of Texas Hill Country-style housing with tin roofs, wood-burning fireplaces, and timber walls. You'd never know the inn is located less than three miles from Fredericksburg's Main Street: The lush greenery, koi pond, and soothing waterfalls allow you to immerse yourself in a peaceful atmosphere.

Thinking about dinner? You don't have to go far for an amazing meal. Cabernet Grill delivers exactly what a Texas Wine Country restaurant should: a service-oriented, chef-driven restaurant with fresh, seasonal offerings, and an impressive all-local wine list—the largest in the state, in fact. Thanks to author, owner and executive chef, Ross Burtwell, the menu offers unique Hill Country cuisine that brings guests back year after year. Think green chile and crab-stuffed shrimp, oak-smoked pork tenderloin, and grilled Texas quail. For dessert? How about Fredericksburg peach crisp with lavender ice cream or chicken-fried pecan pie? Ultra-fresh seafood, Angus beef, and wild game— plus a memorable dessert menu—keep guests happy.

Photographs by Steve Rawls.

2805 S. State Highway 16, Fredericksburg, TX 78264
830.990.8381 cottonginlodging.com

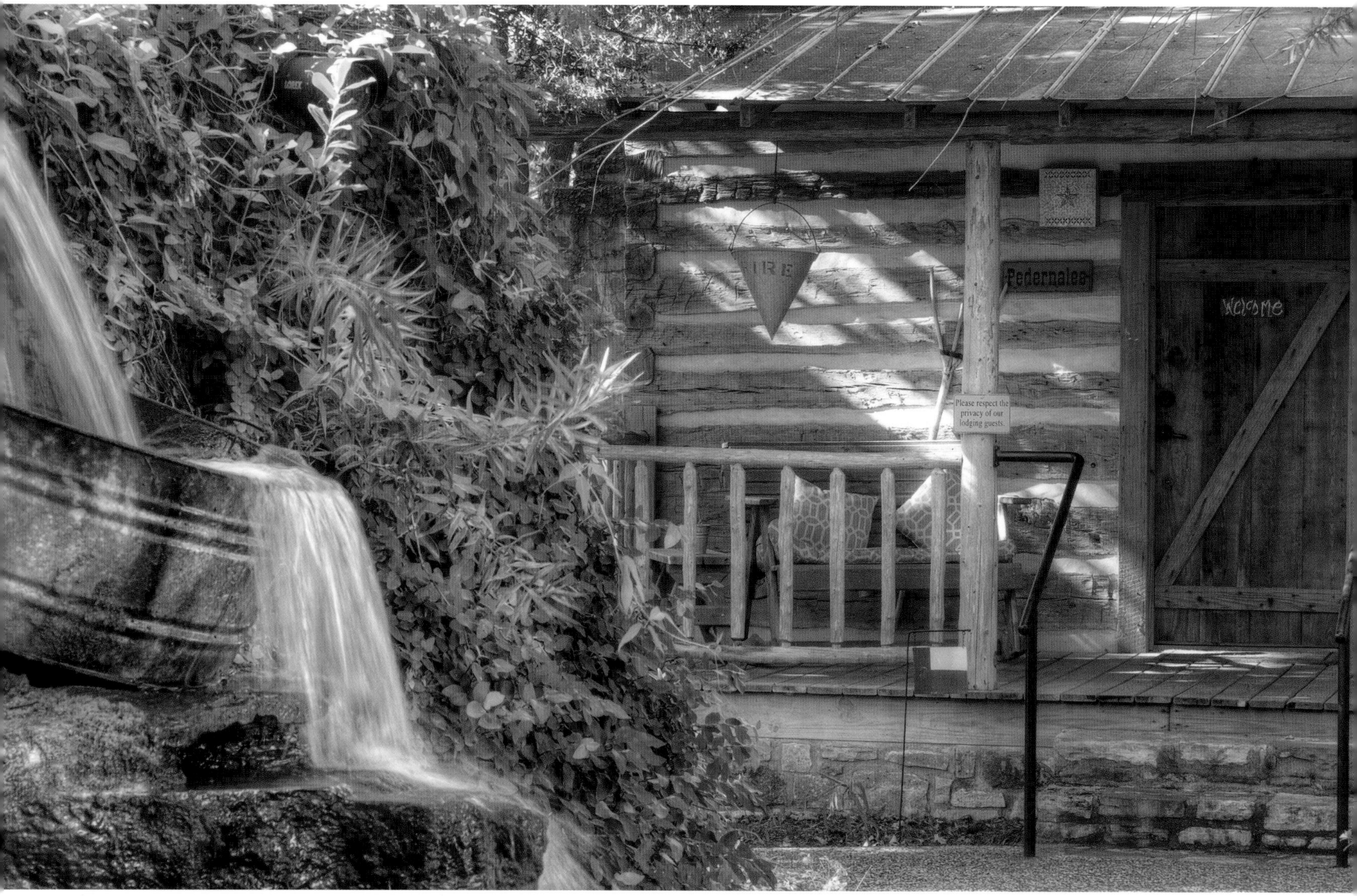
Pedernales
Please respect the privacy of our lodging guests.
Welcome

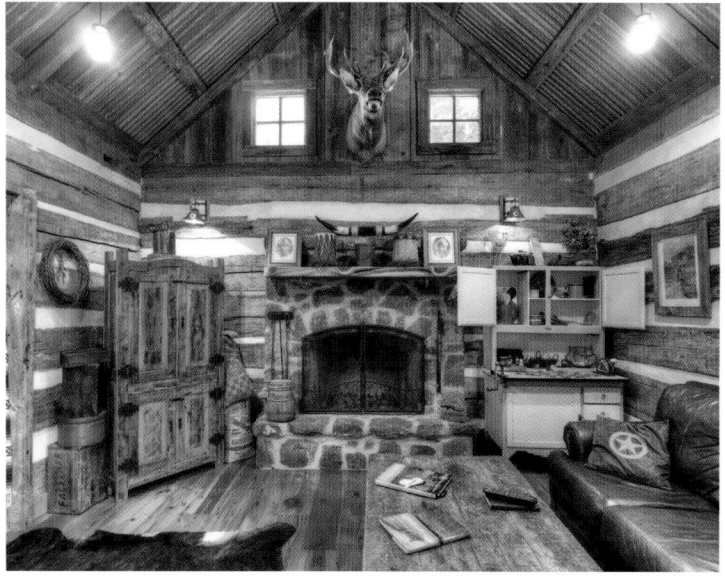

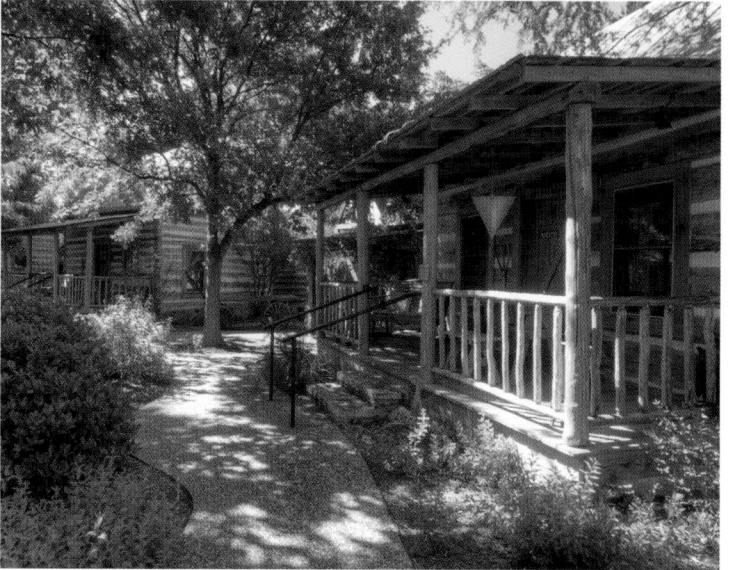

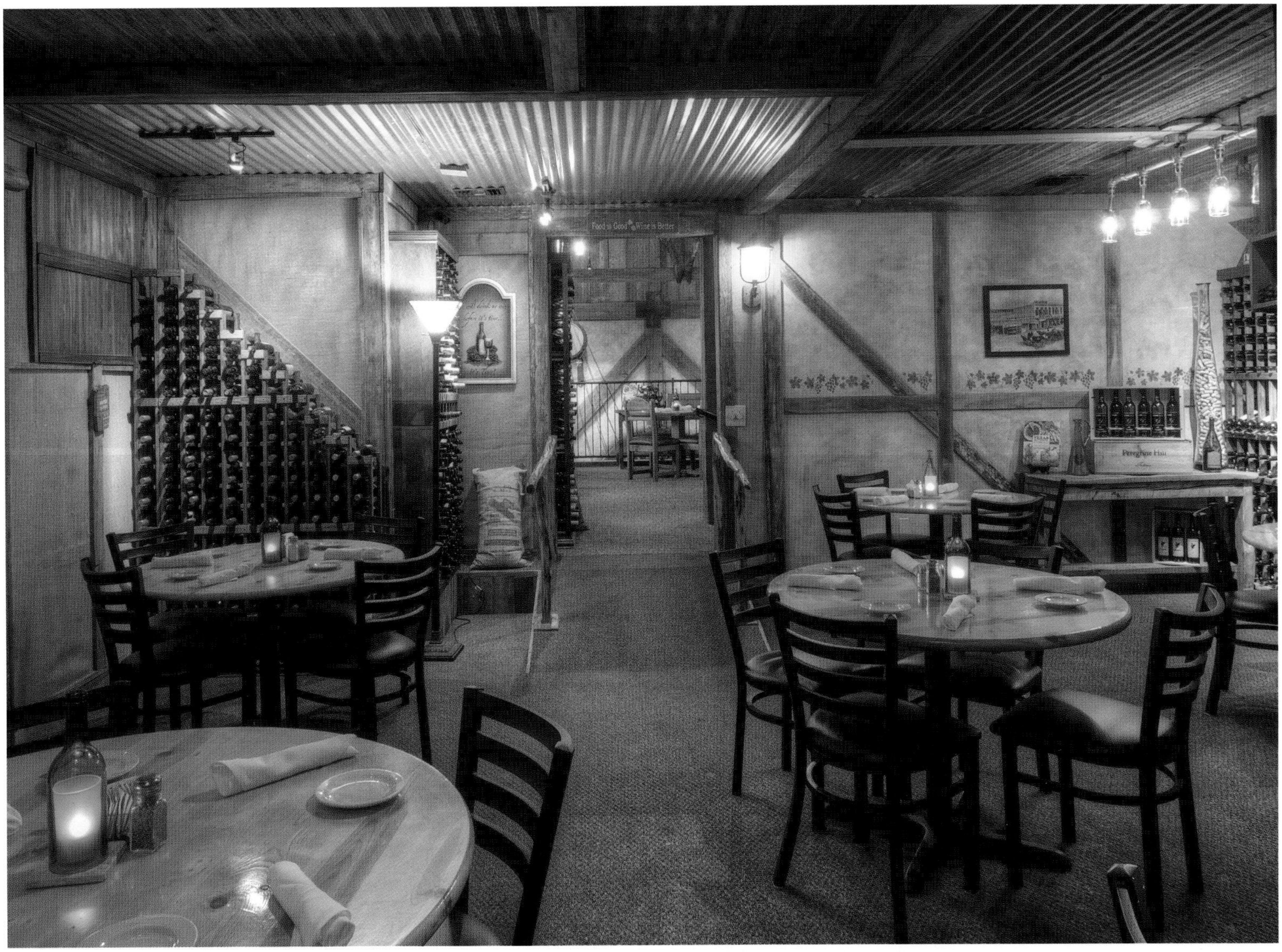
Food is Good Wine is Better

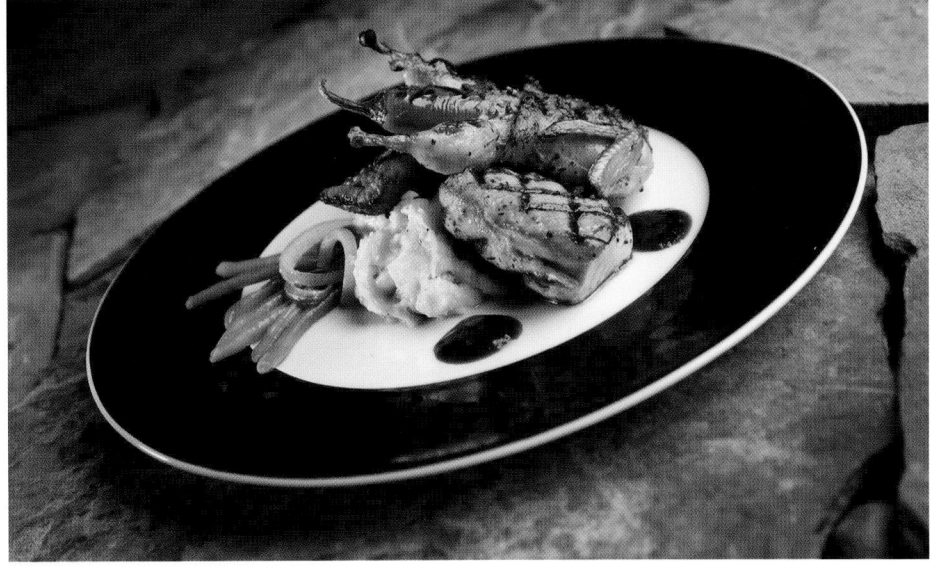

GÄSTEHAUS SCHMIDT

—

spectacular Hill Country lodging

Whether it's a romantic weekend getaway for two, a week-long vacation for 22 of your nearest and dearest—or anything in between—Gästehaus Schmidt has a house, cottage, or suite in town or the country to perfectly fulfill your needs. A family owned business that has been serving the Texas Hill Country since 1985, Gästehaus Schmidt offers more than 125 properties spread throughout Fredericksburg, Comfort, and Ingram. Want to stay in a historic log cabin but also desire to be near all that Main Street has to offer? Then Cay Cay's Cabin is a great option. Just four blocks from Main Street, this romantic residence for two is a real treat. For those who require a bit more space, look no further than Inspiration Hill. Located on a scenic, 10-acre ranch, this home features a spacious, modern kitchen, a multitude of windows with views, and the ability to comfortably sleep nine guests.

Booking couldn't be any easier with the option of booking a stay online through the company's easy-to-use website or calling the toll free number and speaking with a member of the friendly and knowledgeable staff. Looking to make your stay extra special? Gift baskets, flower arrangements, weekend wine tours, and spa days are all just a click or call away.

Photographs by Cyndea Sampson (this page, top, and opposite page, bottom right), D'Ette Cole (opposite page, top), and Sarah Moore (this page, bottom, and opposite page, bottom left).

231 West Main Street, Fredericksburg, TX 78624
866.427.8374 fbglodging.com

HOFFMAN HAUS

—

luxury boutique hotel meets bed & breakfast

If you're looking for a Hill Country getaway that has it all, Hoffman Haus located in Fredericksburg is your ideal destination. Tucked just one block away from the hustle and bustle of historic Main Street, Hoffman Haus is situated in a calm residential neighborhood and strikes the perfect balance between a boutique hotel and a traditional bed & breakfast. With upscale service and serious attention to detail, the Hoffman team creates a memorable Hill Country experience for every visitor. Modern amenities meld gracefully with local traditions. For example, guests can expect a warm gourmet breakfast delivered directly to their rooms in a timeless picnic basket. Vegetarian? Gluten free? Low carb? No problem. The culinary team happily prepares meals to fit any special diet.

Hoffman Haus sits on three beautiful acres and has 23 accommodating spaces—rooms, suites, and cottages—in a variety of styles, all distinct and individually designed by owner Leslie Washburne. While fine linens, soothing colors, and modern bathrooms welcome guests to every room, each space has its own story to tell. The property is a mix of old and new, from the Basse House, constructed in 1871, to the modern details of Ada's Cottage. Hoffman Haus even has an ideal space for events, in its elegant Great Hall—a beautifully restored Kentucky tobacco barn from the 1800s.

Photographs by Claire McCormick.

608 East Creek Street, Fredericksburg, TX 78624
830.997.6739 hoffmanhaus.com

spotlight
KERRVILLE

Kerrville is all about natural beauty. With the Guadalupe River running directly through the heart of downtown, the city is built around the land's stunning assets. The Hill Country gives visitors plenty of options for outdoor adventure: kayaking, fishing, canoeing, biking, or hiking the scenic trails like the ones at Louise Hayes Park. To catch a little bit of it all, head to Riverside Nature Center. Once a small functioning farm, the center is now an urban wildlife and indigenous plant sanctuary. There's walking paths, a wildflower meadow, butterfly gardens, and special programs to check out.

RIVERSIDE NATURE CENTER

150 Francisco Lemos Street, Kerrville, Texas 78028

830.257.4837 riversidenaturecenter.org

Photographs by Jeff Lavender.

MUSEUM OF WESTERN ART

1550 Bandera Highway, Kerrville, Texas 78028

830.896.2553 museumofwesternart.com

Once you're in Kerrville, expect to see fun family activities like the Down by Riverside Festival with native plants for sale, exhibits, and seminars. Easter Fest & Cook-off on the River is another annual event that will have your mouth watering. Celebrate Easter weekend with a barbecue and chili cook-off, plus egg hunts, live entertainment, and contests. If you're looking for indoor, arts and culture-type attractions, Kerrville delivers there, too. Check out the Museum of Western Art, Kathleen C. Cailloux Performing Arts Center, Hill Country Arts Foundation, and Copper Cactus which features handmade furniture, art, and jewelry. Plus there's no shortage of boutique shops and must-try restaurants. To see what's happening in Kerrville, visit kerrvilletexascvb.com.

KATHLEEN C. CAILLOUX PERFORMING ARTS CENTER

910 Main Street, Kerrville, Texas 78028
830.896.9393 caillouxtheater.com

HILL COUNTRY ARTS FOUNDATION

120 Point Theater Road, Ingram, Texas 78025
830.367.5121 hcaf.com

spotlight
LAKE TRAVIS

Tucked deep in the heart of Lakeway and perched above the Rough Hollow Yacht club, Canyon Grille Rough Hollow offers fantastic eats paired with extraordinary views of Lake Travis and breathtaking Hill Country sunsets. Don't mistake the fine food for stuffy pretense. Come as you are to the dining room or spacious patio, choose from the wide selection of dishes, and relax as the experienced staff takes care of the rest.

CANYON GRILLE
103 Yacht Club Cove, Lakeway, TX 78734
512.261.3444 canyongrilleroughhollow.com

Photographs by Photography by Chandi.

Escape the everyday grind, and find yourself immersed in luxury at Spa810. The luxury med spa offers CoolSculpting, injectables including Botox, Juvederm and Kybella, painless laser hair removal, massage therapy, skin care, mineral make-up, and threading. The spa is a modern, sophisticated environment where the best of nature and science are combined to deliver a remarkable experience and to help you look and feel your best.

Family owned and operated, Magpie Blossom Boutique is a full-service floral and gift shop. The family believes in old-fashioned personal service, attention to detail, and a commitment to bringing you unique gifts and floral design. This is not your average floral shop. The boutique is filled with beautiful things, gifts you'll be proud to give, and charming décor to decorate you and your nest.

SPA810

2009 Main Street #200, Lakeway, TX 78734
512.524.9602 spa810.com/austin-lakeway

Photograph by Laurel Belfiore.

MAGPIE BLOSSOM BOUTIQUE

3500 Ranch Road 620 South, Suite F-100, Austin, TX 78738
512.494.6198 magpieblossoms.com

Photograph courtesy of Magpie Blossom Boutique.

HOTEL HAVANA

—

Mediterranean revival on the River Walk

In 1914, local grocer Edward Franz Melcher opened Hotel Havana. He had a vision to recreate the tropical allure of the hotel's Caribbean name-sake, building in the Mediterranean Revival style popular in Cuba at the time. To this day, many of the surrounding cypress, palm, and magnolia trees he planted still remain. In April 2010, Hotel Havana reopened under the humble care of Liz Lambert and her team at Bunkhouse. Situated on a quiet stretch of the North River Walk known as the Museum Reach, Hotel Havana offers elegant accommodations in the heart of San Antonio. The hotel is listed in the National Register of Historic Places but manages to maintain its youthful spirit nonetheless. There are 27 unique rooms and suites available, and the historic property is home to Ocho, a restaurant and lounge offering pan-Latin cuisine. Downstairs, guests can sneak away to the intimate basement bar for a cocktail or two.

Photographs by Nick Simonite.

1015 Navarro Street. San Antonio. TX 78205
210.222.2008 havanasanantonio.com

HOTEL VALENCIA RIVERWALK

—

River Walk hotel that has it all

From meetings and business trips on the River Walk to romantic getaways or weddings—whatever your reason for visiting—Hotel Valencia Riverwalk will make your San Antonio trip one to remember.

The team takes pride in delivering an impeccable experience rather than a routine hotel stay. The architectural craftsmanship and opulent finishes throughout the design of the building envelop your senses while luxury amenities cater to your every need. With world-class dining and in-room spa services, you may find it difficult to leave at all during your stay, but if you do, a bevy of options are just steps away.

Steeped in history and charm, the hotel blends Spanish Colonial and modern Mediterranean design with contemporary ideals. The downtown location—nestled in on the quiet part of the River Walk—keeps you in the middle of the action without sacrificing tranquility. Surround yourself with dining, entertainment, and shopping offered along the vibrant banks of the famed River Walk, or visit nearby local attractions. Embrace the romance of the downtown architecture as you tour the area by horse-drawn carriage or river cruise. However you choose to spend your time in San Antonio, Hotel Valencia Riverwalk will ensure it's unforgettable.

Photographs by Jerry Hayes.

150 East Houston, San Antonio, TX 78205
210.748.7462 hotelvalencia-riverwalk.com

CLIFF HAVEN ON THE GUADALUPE

—

private Hill Country escape
high above the Guadalupe River

Why would you travel like a tourist when you can visit like a local? Cliff Haven on the Guadalupe sits on a limestone cliff above the river, and this unique guesthouse offers you the chance to feel like you have a personal Hill Country vacation home. With sweeping vistas of the surrounding terrain, this house was designed for rest, relaxation, and fun. It's conveniently located near shopping, dining, and outdoor activities, yet still feels like it's in the middle of nowhere. Bask in a warm fire from the stone fire pit in the evenings, surrounded by the walls of the courtyard, or take in the views from the private pool and spa.

The house is located on two-and-a-half acres in a safe and quiet community in Spring Branch. You can use it as a home away from home to visit the Hill Country, New Braunfels, and San Antonio, or just stay and unwind. The two-bedroom, two-bathroom home sleeps up to five people and features modern, Mexican rustic, and Texas chic décor. Your favorite space will be the Texas living room: a finished-out garage with air conditioning, a full bathroom, a mini refrigerator, billiards table, and everything else you need for the ultimate hangout spot. The best part? You can take in the killer views while you relax, thanks to the all-glass garage door.

Photographs by Shoot2Sell.

2116 Whispering Water, Spring Branch, TX 78070
210.391.9240 vrbo.com/967283

134

MIGEL HOUSE

—

sophisticated relaxation in the heart of Texas

The Migel House has undoubtedly stood the test of time. Changing and adapting over the years, the structure remains as beautiful and appealing today as when it was first built in 1910. You can almost picture the opulent garden parties and lavish social events that took place when Louis Migel—a successful department store owner—occupied the home in the Roaring '20s. Originally funded by an investor named Nelson Smith, the home was designed and built by Milton M. Scott, one of the region's top architects of his time.

Today, the half-acre garden spaces and comfortable accommodations show off all the historic details, beautifully preserved and on display for visitors to enjoy. Stained glass windows, restored wainscoting, and original wood floors maintain the home's character and turn-of-the-century appeal. Guests have some difficult choices for their Waco stay at the Migel House. Opt for the Louey Suite and spoil yourself with heated floors, king-size bed, and a relaxing balcony. Or pick the Carriage House and get a quiet space with a full kitchen and walk-in shower—close to the Brazos Riverwalk and night life.

Photographs by James Brown (opposite, top) and Marcel Van Es Photography (all others).

1425 Columbus Avenue, Waco, TX 76701
254.523.6611 migelhouse.com

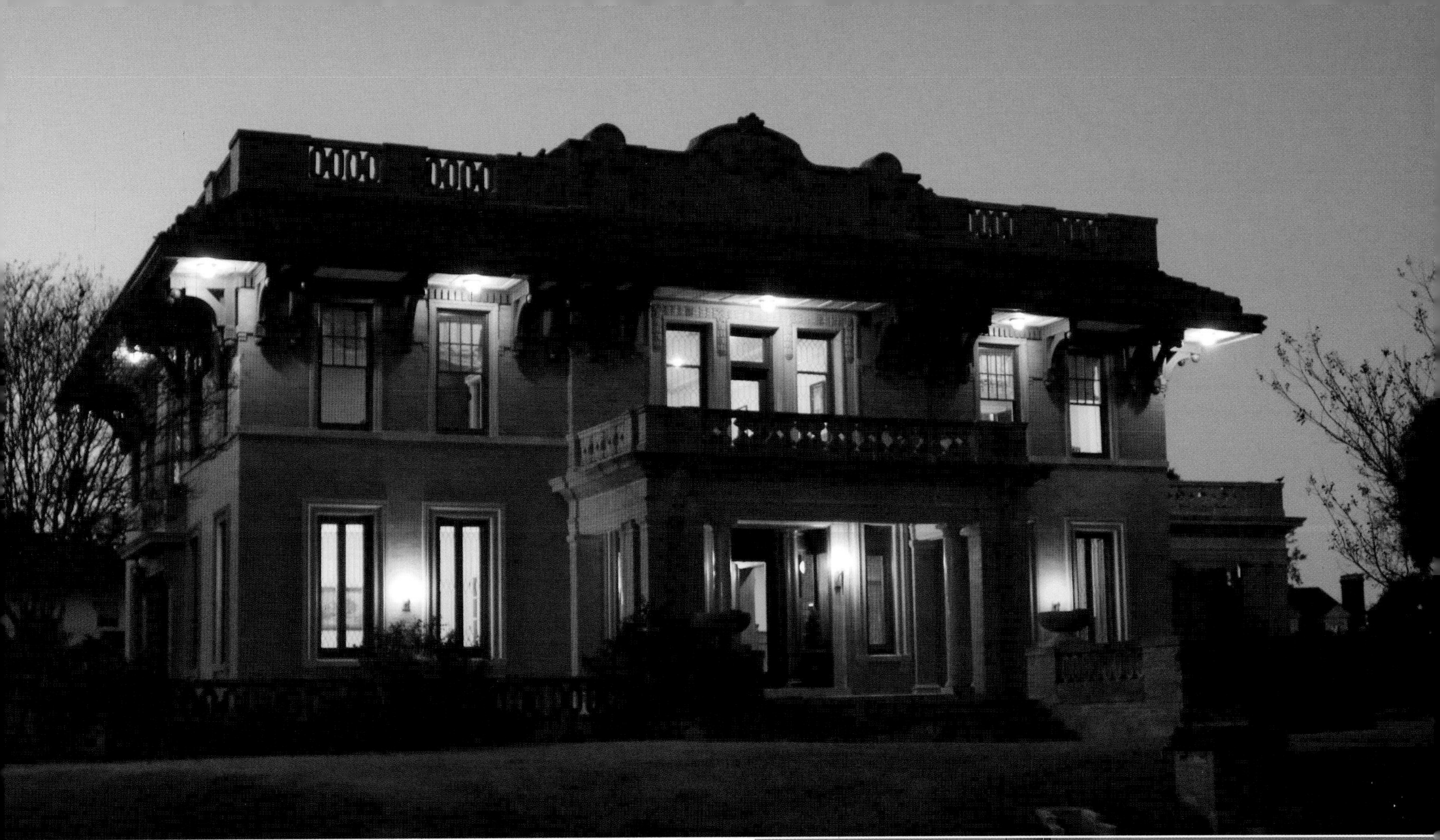

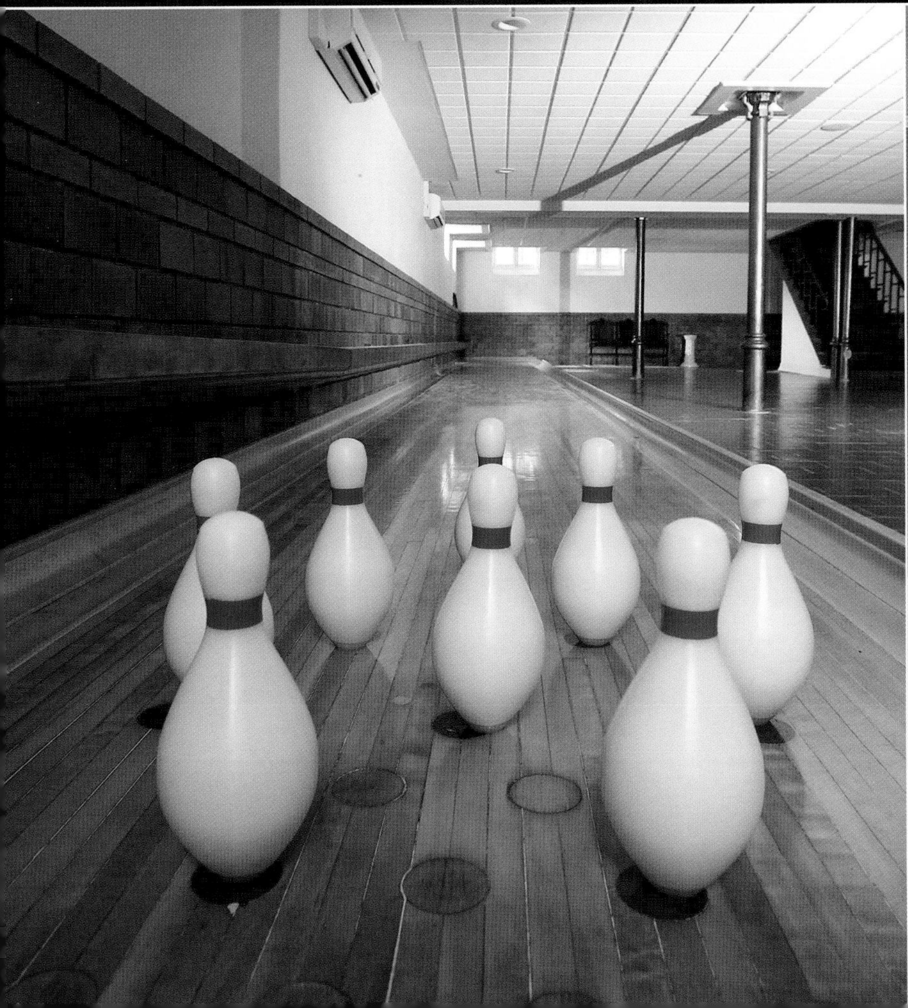

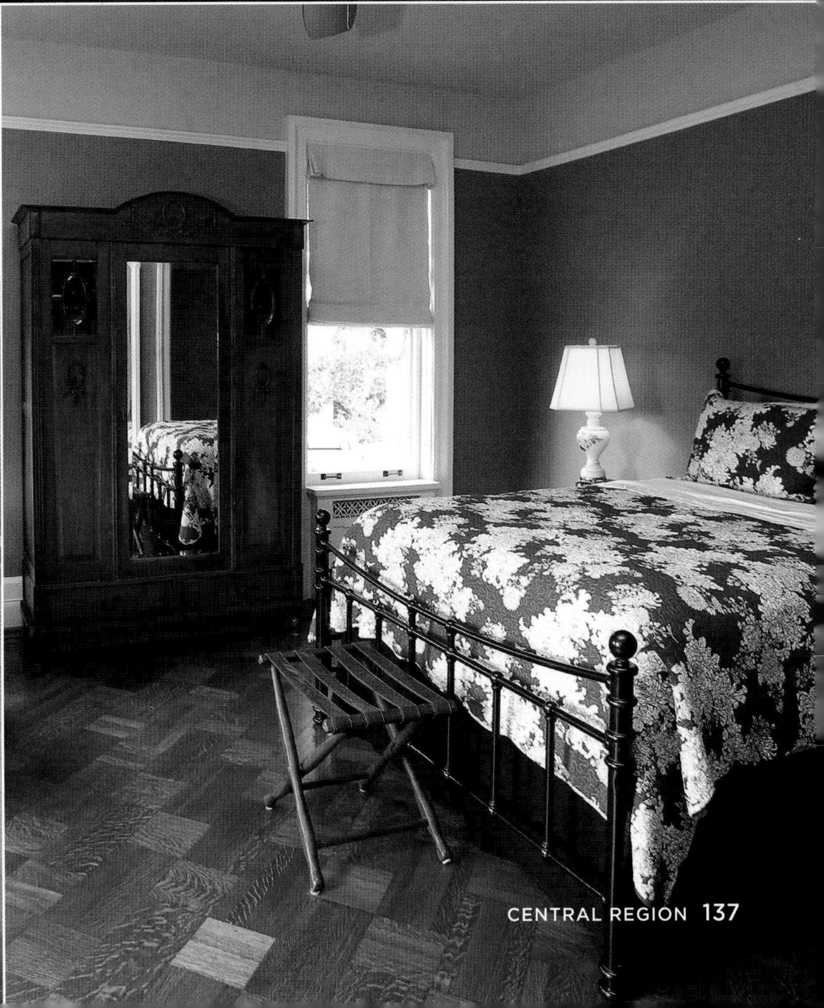

Southeastern Region

Gulf Shrimp boats at the dock
Photograph courtesy of Texas Shrimp Marketing Program.

USS Lexington aircraft carrier in Corpus Christi
Photograph courtesy of Corpus Christi CVB..

Historic Jackson Street in Harlingen
Photograph courtesy of Rodrigo Davila.

Downtown Bastrop
Photograph courtesy of City of Bastrop.

Sample Road Trip
Start: Bastrop
End: Kemah
Miles: 166

Rise and shine then head straight to Bastrop's gorgeous Main Street. Have fun looking in the shops and trying out the culinary treasures. Drive through **Bastrop State Park** and marvel at the Lost Pines. Carry on down the road to the bustling city of Houston—the fourth largest city in the nation. Stay in a quaint Bed & Breakfast on a quiet tree-lined street. **Uphouse Manor** has super-comfy beds and is just walking distance to many attractions. End the day wining and dining at Houston's famous **Papas Bros. Steakhouse**. You will want to spend your first full day in town shopping at **The Galleria or Highland Village**, where you'll find retail that runs the gamet from vintage to high-end designer. If shopping is not your thing, explore the **Museum District** or head down to the **Space Center Houston**. You can actually have lunch with a NASA astronaut on Fridays and Saturdays! Escape the cosmopolitan life and scoot over to the sweet town of **Kemah**, located on the breezy shores of Galveston Bay. Check into the waterfront boutique hotel, **The Boardwalk Inn**. Stroll around the famous Kemah Boardwalk—the sprawling entertainment complex with waterfront dining, theme park rides, plus a stingray touch pool and rainforest exhibit. For the wine lovers, try **Clear Creek Vineyard** for a wine tasting experience you'll never forget. The fun never stops.

Conroe is home to three award-winning craft breweries: B-52 Brewing Company, Southern Star, and Copperhead. Southern Star's claim to fame? It was the first to can craft beer in the state of Texas. All three breweries offer tours and tastings throughout the week with third-party beer buses available to transport patrons between each of the breweries.

Crighton Theatre is a historic performing arts center and former Vaudeville stage that opened in 1934 and now hosts several theater companies. It's home to the Stage Right production company and The Sounds of Texas Music Series, and is also known throughout the industry for its perfect acoustics.

B-52 BREWING COMPANY
12470 Milroy Lane, Conroe, TX 77304
936.447.4677 b52.com

Photographs by Steve Basham, PSC Video Services.

CRIGHTON THEATRE
234 North Main Street, Conroe, TX 77301
936.441.7469 crightontheatre.org

Extending 21 miles and covering 22,000 surface acres, Lake Conroe is the reserve drinking water supply for the city of Houston and offers clean, clear water for a variety of recreation: boating, fishing, hunting, golfing, swimming, water skiing, and jet skiing. Luxurious hotels and condominiums, top-notch RV parks, boat storage with valet launching, and stunning waterfront real estate developments are only a few of the attractions on this manmade lake.

The Lone Star Monument and Historical Flag Park showcases Montgomery County as the birthplace of the Lone Star Flag. Towering battle and rally flags depict those that flew during Texas' fight for independence. A 14-foot bronze statue known as The Texian, conceived and sculpted by artist Craig Campobella, serves as the centerpiece. A bronze bust dedicated to Dr. Charles B. Stewart, the Montgomery County native credited with the design of the Lone Star Flag, greets visitors at the park entrance.

WATERPOINT MARINA ON LAKE CONROE

15264 TX-105, Montgomery, TX 77356
936.788.2628 waterpointmarina.com

LONE STAR MONUMENT AND FLAG PARK

212 Interstate 45 North, Conroe, TX 77301
936.522.3842 texasflagpark.com

BELLE OAKS INN

—

hidden treasure in historic Gonzales

Not too far from any major Texas city lies an undiscovered gem: the town of Gonzales. You may have driven through this spot on your way to Houston or San Antonio, but what you didn't realize is that Gonzales is a destination in itself. Nestled just 10 miles off Interstate 10, you'll find Belle Oaks Inn—the ideal place to stay and see the town. The Greek Revival mansion was built in 1912 and has been completely restored and updated, now offering visitors elegant accommodations. Each of the seven guest suites has a distinct, individual style and has been carefully appointed for comfort and convenience. With lush grounds, historic details, and elegant finishes, you really have to see the inn to appreciate its beauty.

Gonzales has a little something for everyone—fine dining, antique shops, a rodeo arena, and golf courses—but history lovers will be particularly entertained here. Known as the birthplace of Texas independence, the town features dozens of historically significant spots. There is a historical marker at nearby Cost where the first shots of the Texas Revolution were fired, the Memorial Museum, Texas Heroes Square, and Pioneer Village to name a few.

Photographs by Tre Dunham of Fine Focus Photography (opposite page), and Clint Hille (this page).

222 St. Peter Street, Gonzales, TX 78629
830.857.8613 belleoaksinn.com

spotlight
GONZALES

Nothing quite captures the rebellious, historical spirit of Gonzales like the Come and Take It Celebration. The annual festival lasts three days and happens on the first full weekend in October to commemorate the anniversary of the first shots fired in Texas' fight for independence. Guests can expect live music, a battle reenactment, tasty food, a car show, and plenty of activities for the kids.

COME AND TAKE IT CELEBRATION

Historic Downtown Gonzales, Gonzales, TX 78629

830.672.6532 gonzalestexas.com

Photograph by Erik McCowan.

Take a step back in time at Pioneer Village Living History Center—a collection of homes and buildings that have been preserved from the 1800s and are open for visitors to tour. Texas enthusiasts and history buffs will love this authentic, preserved peek into everyday life from long ago. During the first two weekends of December, experience Pioneer Village's largest event, Stars in the Village.

PIONEER VILLAGE LIVING HISTORY CENTER

2122 North St. Joseph Street, Gonzales, TX 78629

830.672.2157 thepioneervillage.vpweb.com

Photograph by Yellow Horse Designs.

Sponsored by the Gonzales Historic Homes Association and Gonzales Chamber, the beloved annual Historic Homes Tour lets spectators see some of the town's most beautiful residential architecture. You'll walk into various centuries of decor and celebration; it's an experience you can feel good about. All proceeds go towards beautification and historic preservation efforts.

GONZALES HISTORIC HOMES TOUR

414 St. Lawrence, Gonzales, TX 78629

830.672.6532 gonzalestexas.com

Photograph by Daisy Scheske Freeman.

Gonzales Memorial Museum is a beautiful Art Deco complex constructed of shell and Cordova limestone. There are two exhibition wings, a large outdoor amphitheater, and a reflecting pool. Guests can view period rifles, ammunition, uniform, physician's tools, and what is arguably the original "Come and take it" cannon. To get details on this and all the other cool things to do in Gonzales, visit Gonzalestexas.com.

GONZALES MEMORIAL MUSEUM

414 Smith Street, Gonzales, TX 78629

830.672.6350 gonzales.texas.gov

Photograph by Gerri Lawing.

spotlight
SHOP GONZALES

A little tough, a little feminine, and totally Texas, Angels & Outlaws has clothes for people who love the Lone Star State. The boutique shop sells women's clothing, jewelry, shoes, accessories, and there's even a few options for children and men. Proud of their slightly crooked halos, the founders are two lifelong best friends who have a deep-seeded commitment to each other and the business. They want women everywhere to show some grit and look good while doing it.

ANGELS & OUTLAWS

413 St. George Street, Gonzales, TX 78629

830.263.4124 angelsandoutlaws.biz

Photograph by Ainsley Joseph.

Pop into Sweet B's and choose from pies, cookies, cupcakes, and truffles, plus an adorable retail section with baker's goodies like aprons and kitchen items. Started by a young entrepreneur, the bakery specializes in decorated cookies and custom cakes. Try the homemade ice cream, and if you want to eat like a local, opt for the Big Red flavor—it's the town favorite.

SWEET B'S

521 St. Joseph Street, Gonzales, TX 78629

830.519.4040 facebook.com/sweetbsdessert

Photograph by Courtney Rea Photography.

Main St. Marketplace has all the cool things you didn't know you needed. The vintage-themed shop sells collectibles and antiques in nearly every category: furniture, jewelry, wall décor, kitchen goodies, and memorabilia. It also has cool events like art classes, wine tastings, and makeup parties.

MAIN ST. MARKETPLACE

515 North St. Joseph Street, Gonzales, TX 78629
830.519.4023
facebook.com/Main-Street-Market-Place-104729096543951/

Photograph by Willow & Fern.

Fall in love with Laurel Ridge Inn, Antiques, Christmas & Gifts, where it's Christmas all year. From *Come and Take It* until December 25, Laurel Ridge is dripping with Christmas. Year-round you can shop exquisite estate and custom jewelry, antique furniture and art, flowers galore, and, of course, Christmas. You can even spend the night in the historic 1914 property.

LAUREL RIDGE CHRISTMAS, ANTIQUES & HISTORIC INN

827 St. Joseph Street, Gonzales, TX 78629
830.672.2484 laurelridgegonzales.com

Photograph courtesy of Laurel Ridge.

UPHOUSE MANOR

—

tailored escape in the heart of Houston Heights

On a tree-lined residential street in the historic section of the Heights, Uphouse Manor offers guests an exceptional getaway experience. Built in 1908, the manor thrives as a stunning piece of heritage surrounded by the vibrant local cultural scene. The interior style is a beautiful mix of reclaimed elements and modern amenities, with touches of industrial. Breakfast is specially crafted with whole and organic foods and always includes the freshest ingredients. Seasonal produce, cultural selections, and dietary restrictions are all given consideration in preparing your menu.

Owner and operator Katrina Price Stilwell is a local interior designer who shares her flair for curating spaces for clients throughout the Houston area. Driven to share the beauty of the Heights, Katrina welcomes road warriors, locals, love birds, families, and events to the manor. Visitors can hang out on one of the porches overlooking the gardens, or take advantage of the tempting robes, fluffy towels, organic soaps, and relaxing clawfoot tubs in the rooms. Quietly recline with a book or laptop, or accept an invitation to a glass of wine or marshmallow roasting at the chiminea. Come home to Uphouse.

Photographs by Frederick Warren Photography, LLC.

235 West 18th Street, Houston, TX 77008
832.786.9867 uphousemanor.com

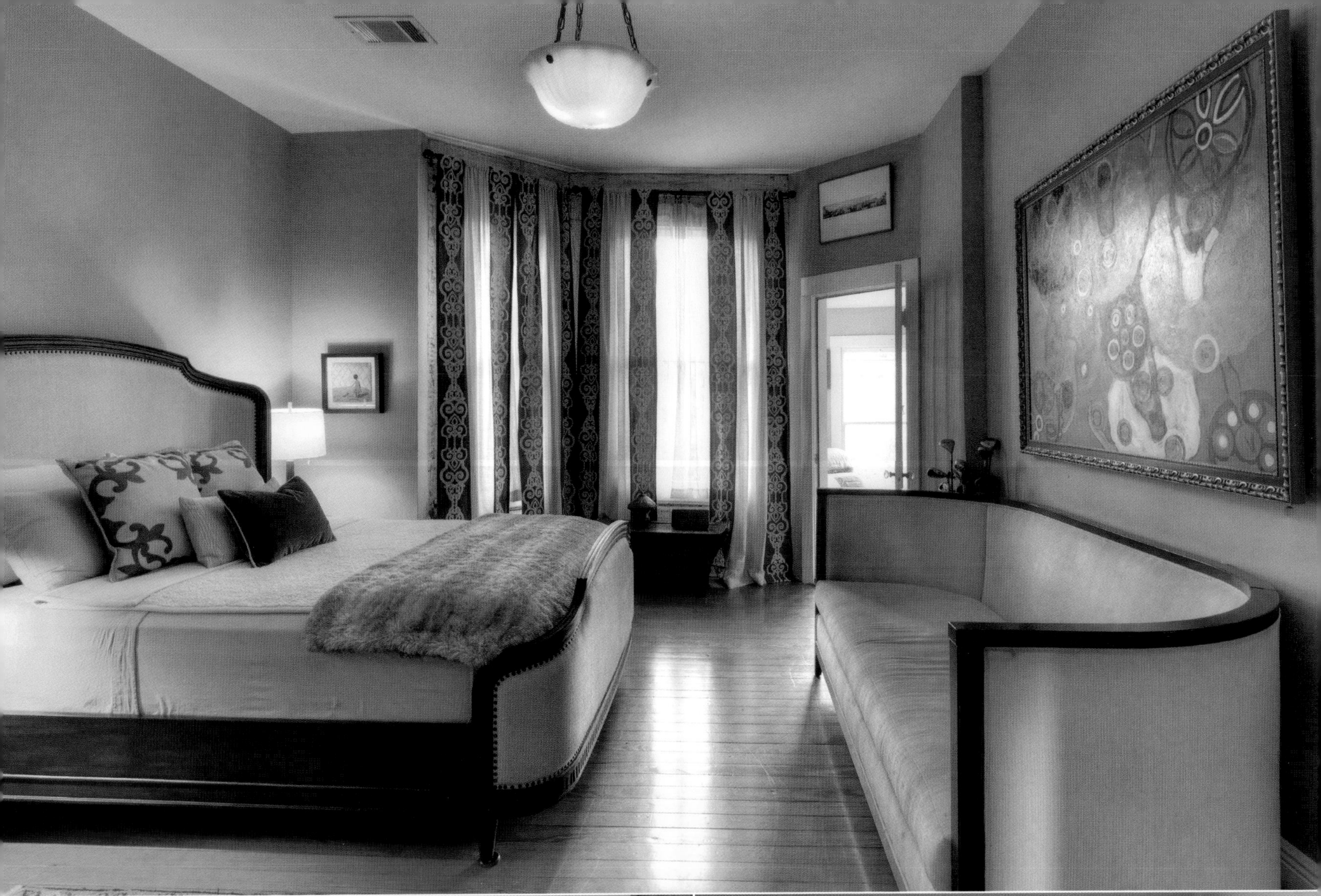

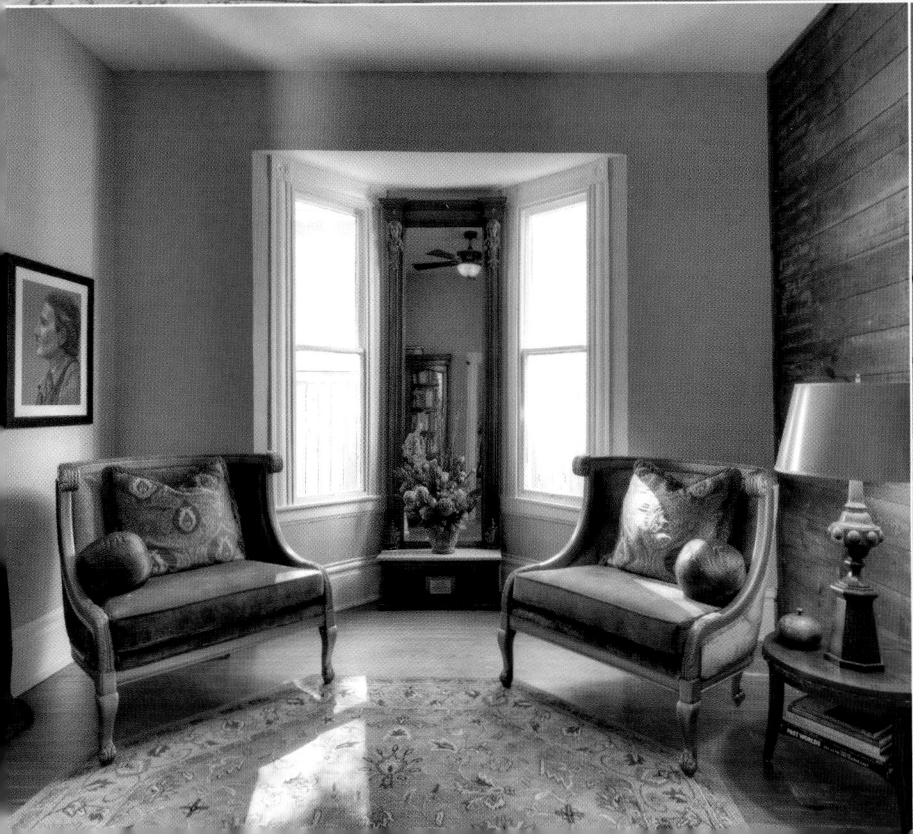

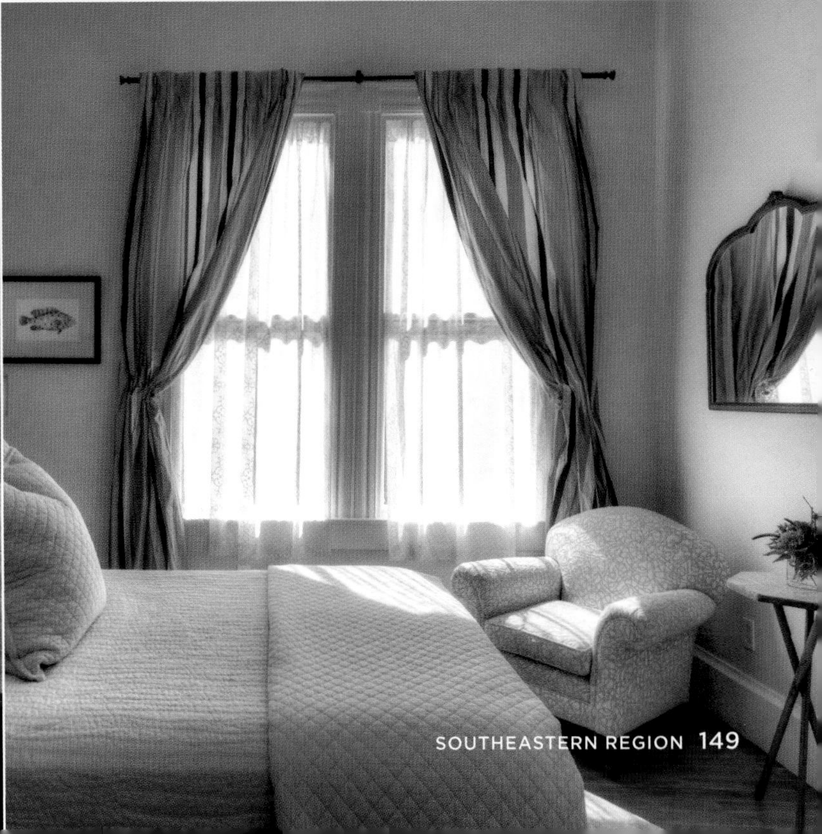

CLIPPER HOUSE INN

—

tranquil inn and winery with a restaurant you'll never forget

Although the Clipper House Inn is just blocks from Kemah's bustling boardwalk, you'd never know it. The 1920s cottages and lush gardens are quiet, peaceful, and feel like a tranquil escape from the busy world. Beautifully appointed, the accommodations show off antique furniture and vintage decor from the proprietary families'—the Skinners and the Hoppers—world travels. Amenities include luxurious bathrooms, Egyptian-cotton towels, and exquisite 500-thread count sheets and linens.

Guests can enjoy the onsite demonstration vineyard for the nearby Clear Creek Winery as well as the beautiful garden courtyard. As part of the Clipper House family, the three-story elevated winery offers complimentary tours to the inn's guests and an impressive wine tasting welcome. Clear Creek has a well-rounded list of award-winning varietals to try. Attached to the winery is Eculent Restaurant, and it's unlike any you've seen before. The 16-seat dining room has one seating per night and gives visitors a multisensory, choreographed meal, complete with customized lighting, scents, soundtrack, and changing artwork. One of only three like it in the world, the restaurant offers a tour of the kitchen and food lab before dinner. It's an unforgettable experience.

Photographs by Ran DeBord (this page) and David Skinner (opposite page).

710 Bradford Avenue, Kemah, TX 77565
281.334.2517 clipperhouseinn.com

spotlight
KEMAH

Kemah is an American Indian word meaning "wind in my face" and captures the carefree spirit of the city. Come "breeze into Kemah," a slogan that accurately describes the recreational environment of the waterfront town. The city is appropriately named, as it's near a constant ocean breeze from Galveston Bay. Kemah's name has also been long associated with seaside fun and living it up on the Texas Coast.

That's never been more true than today, with the spectacular Kemah Boardwalk and Kemah Waterfront District offering a variety of shops, fine restaurants, and marinas with just about any kind of water-related activity you can imagine. Kemah is Texas' spot to just relax and take a break. Located just 25 minutes south of Houston and 25 minutes north of Galveston, the town is an ideal central getaway for southeastern Texas. Kemah has approximately 1,800 residents but hosts more than four million visitors each year from all over the state and across the country. That's partly in thanks to the cool events, fun festivals, amusement park, and great night life, but mostly because of Kemah's warm, welcoming spirit. Plan your getaway at visitbayareahouston.com.

Photographs by Wali Muhammad (opposite page, far right) and T FOTEH Photography (all others).

One of the Texas coast's top marinas

Kemah's Boardwalk, a favorite Texas getaway

An amusement park with something for everyone

Fun on the water: boating, fishing, kayaking, and so much more

Beautiful monuments to marine life

SOUTH SHORE HARBOUR RESORT

—

seaside serenity just outside of Houston

South Shore Harbour Resort and Conference Center's multi-million-dollar renovation has brought a "new look, new experience" to Bay Area Houston's waterfront. The swimming area has been restructured as The Oasis, an expanded resort pool with cabanas and a swim-up bar. Also new, the Lighthouse Bar & Bistro has elegant décor and dramatic views of the sunset over the marina. Public areas, suites, and 232 guestrooms have new upscale, modern décor. "We are surrounded by America's third-largest recreational boating area, golf courses and a 130,000-square-foot fitness center with a full-service spa," says general manager Roy Green.

Amenities include luxury suites, an exclusive executive floor, free covered parking with elevator access to guest rooms, and secure wireless internet. Guests can conveniently get to Hobby Airport, cruise ships, and two championship golf courses from the resort. The historic shops at League City are also nearby, as well as the marina where dinner cruises and fishing expeditions depart from. The popular Kemah Boardwalk, NASA's Mission Control Center, Space Center Houston, and Galveston Island aren't too far either, along with Armand Bayou Nature Preserve, museums, and many more attractions.

2500 South Shore Boulevard, League City, TX 77573
281.334.1000 sshr.com

STARHILL FARMS

—

storied farm with rustic comfort

Nestled in the Mill Creek Valley, StarHill Farms is set on 300 rolling acres. It's beautiful, relaxing, and the perfect place to sneak away for a long weekend. Perhaps the most intriguing aspect of StarHill Farms is its history. The property was included in the original part of Stephen F. Austin's land grant from the Mexican government and settled primarily by German and Czechoslovakian immigrants. Among them were Friedrich and Julia Sternenberg, or Sternberg, who arrived in Texas in 1850. They purchased the StarHill Farms property from Bryant Daughtrey who was granted the land from the Mexican government as part of Stephen F. Austin's second colony. Carl Otto Sternenberg bought the property in 1877 and helped create the StarHill (that's Sternenberg in German) Community.

Today, the property is owned by the Frappier family. They bought the home in 1996 and have been on a mission to restore all its original charm and historical elements. The restoration includes four log cabins and a ranch house. The Cabin on the Hill is a fully renovated cabin that overlooks Mill Creek and features customized fixtures, reclaimed wood, hand-selected antiques, and stone work. With its rich history and impressive accommodations, StarHill Farms take you to the heart and soul of Texas.

Photographs by Gary Lankford.

2038 Iris Lane, New Ulm, TX 78950
713.524.2638. starhillfarms.com

CINNAMON SHORE

—

*charming seaside community
that draws families together*

On the outskirts of Port Aransas, there's a new kind of beachside destination waiting to be discovered. Bringing new urbanism to the Texas Coast when it debuted in 2007, the resort community of Cinnamon Shore offers all the hallmarks you'd expect for a coastal development. You'll find paver sidewalks that wind along palm-lined streets, charming residences with serious porch appeal, a respected bistro that invites conversations over drinks, pocket parks, and shared green spaces such as the Great Lawn.

Cinnamon Shore has matured into a complete community with 200-plus homes, townhomes, and condos. It has charmed vacationers and second-home owners from Dallas, Houston, Austin, and San Antonio, and feels a bit like a well-kept secret. The breezy seaside village is nestled into protective dunes, and the community beckons seekers of relaxation, romance, and family fun. The Town Center has a mixed-use, small-town vibe and features a pizzeria and fresh market. You'll find nautical rentals, scenic pools, fine dining, equipment rentals like golf carts and large beach umbrellas, concierge services, and tons of cool activities like sandcastle-building lessons and beach yoga.

Photographs courtesy of Cinnamon Shore.

5009 Highway 361, Port Aransas, TX 78373
866.639.9919 cinnamonshore.com

spotlight
PORT ARANSAS
AND MUSTANG ISLAND

Port Aransas and Mustang Island are 18 miles of wide, sandy beaches, and everything you seek for the perfect island escape. But this is no ordinary island—just ask the locals and vacationers who've treasured it for decades. You'll find year-round outdoor activities from sport fishing and parasailing to birding, dolphin watching, kayaking, and the only links-style golf course in Texas. Stroll through town on a golf cart, explore the shops and galleries, or enjoy an array of dining options from "cook your catch" to Texas barbecue—but it doesn't stop there. You'll find year-round festivals and events, including the burgeoning Port A Live music scene, Beachtoberfest, Whooping Crane Festival, and Texas SandFest. With a new wave of luxurious seaside vacation homes, cottages, hotels, or glamping sites, you can find the perfect place to accommodate every lifestyle and budget.

One of the few destinations that has something for everyone, Port Aransas and Mustang Island are favorites for many. Start planning your visit at visitportaransas.com today, or download the new Visit Port Aransas and Mustang Island mobile app so you can explore everything the island offers.

Photographs courtesy of Port Aransas/Mustang Island Chamber of Commerce & Tourism Bureau.

Island sunrises that are second to none

Sweeping views of the coast

A beach bike ride in the coastal breeze

Serious sand architecture at Texas SandFest

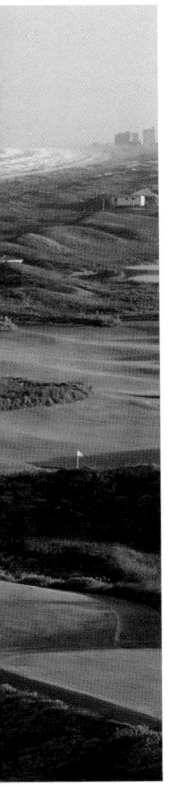

Romantic seaside dining

ANGEL ROSE BED & BREAKFAST

—

seaside Victorian charmer

It's hard to guess which part of Angel Rose Bed & Breakfast you'll love the most: the cool ocean breeze, the unforgettable front porch, or the fresh homemade breakfasts. Fully remodeled, this seaside Victorian home has maintained all of its charm and character from when it was built in 1881. Originally constructed with French Regency design and remodeled in 1910, Angel Rose now features a gabled roof, yellow cypress siding, long-leaf pine floors, and its legendary wrap-around porch. The family of the original owners were an integral part of the first German settlements in Texas. Today, Rusty and Jennifer Day own and operate the bed & breakfast and have focused on warm Southern hospitality, maintaining the integrity of the home, and providing guests with an amazing night's sleep and gourmet breakfast. You've got to try their signature pecan pie muffins.

The rooms are elegantly appointed with vintage furniture, period antiques, and private baths with claw-foot tubs. Featuring a king-size bed and private bathroom, the Iris Room has a producing mango tree just outside the window. Upstairs, the Rose Room has a calming floral theme and offers a queen-size bed, a private bathroom, and a view of the bay. The Violet Room, also on the second floor, offers a pillow-top queen-size bed and private bath.

Bicycle rentals are available for cruising around Rockport's arts district, museums, beachfronts, historical sites, and old Main Street shopping areas.

Photograph by Maria Nesbit.

902 E. Cornwall Street, Rockport, TX 78382
361.729.3189 angelrosebb.com

spotlight
SCHULENBURG

When you see images of the Schulenburg-area painted churches, you'd never guess that they sit quietly in small southeastern Texas communities. They look more like something you'd see in Europe. The 19th-century structures were built and painted by German and Czech immigrants and appear all around Schulenburg: Dubina, Praha, and further out in Fredericksburg. Breathtaking colors and Gothic architecture make these churches memorable and tell the stories of the communities they're in and the people who built them. Although the churches have active parishes, they are available for visitors to tour and enjoy. Contact the Schulenburg Chamber of Commerce for more information.

If you're still craving more Texas history, the local museum tour is sure to satisfy. It includes the Texas Polka Museum, the Schulenburg Historical Museum, and the Stanzel Model Aircraft Museum and gives visitors insight into the significance of the region. There is also the County Line Tour that offers a mix-and-match option of churches and museums. Wine enthusiasts will find a pleasant surprise on their visit to Schulenburg, with several local wineries worth checking out. Head to Moravia, Majek, and Whistling Duck vineyards and wineries for the perfect way to enjoy authentic Texas wine and fresh, local fare.

Photographs by Christina Pereyda (top row) and Sami Hall (bottom left and center), and courtesy of Schulenburg Chamber of Commerce (bottom right).

Stunning painted churches of Schulenburg

Lush green vineyards

Wines at Moravia Vineyard & Winery

Historic log cabins at Wolter's Park

spotlight
THE WOODLANDS

Wouldn't you love to see a concert at a top-ranked amphitheater? You can in The Woodlands. The Cynthia Woods Mitchell Pavilion will not disappoint music lovers. Top acts have toured here, including the Goo Goo Dolls, Jimmy Buffet, John Mayer, Kings of Leon, and so many more.

There's no better way to see The Woodlands than by kayak. Choose to travel tandem or solo and check out the bars, restaurants, and lush surroundings as you cruise through the water. Visitors can choose group games or opt for a date package. There's also a picnic pack available—a great option for families.

THE CYNTHIA WOODS MITCHELL PAVILION
2005 Lake Robbins Drive, The Woodlands, TX 77380
281.364.3010 woodlandscenter.org

Photograph by Ted Washington.

RIVA ROW BOATHOUSE
2101 Riva Row, The Woodlands, TX 77380
281.210.3965 thewoodlandstownship-tx.gov/rivarowboathouse

Photograph by Ashton Rodgers.

Looking for a little bit of everything? Market Street has top retail stores and the best restaurants. Think Kendra Scott, Tiffany & Co., Trina Turk, Cru Food & Wine Bar, and Jasper's Backyard Gourmet Cuisine. Visitors can get all the perks of big-city shopping and dining without the hassle.

Nature enthusiasts, this is your stop. Montgomery County has worked hard to maintain the beauty of its land and invites guests to check out the preserve, part of the Spring Creek Greenway. There are miles of beautiful biking and hiking, along with bird watching, fishing, and plenty of local history.

MARKET STREET

9595 Six Pines Drive, The Woodlands, TX 77380

281.419.4774 marketstreet-thewoodlands.com

Photograph by Derrick Bryant.

THE GEORGE MITCHELL NATURE PRESERVE

5171 Flintridge Drive, The Woodlands, TX 77381

281.353.8100 springcreekgreenway.org

Photograph by Ashton Rodgers.

VINTAGE SOUTHERN COMFORT

—

Brenham charmer with real Southern appeal

At Vintage Southern Comfort, Southern is a way of life—sweet tea, porch sitting, slow sunsets, and the best hospitality in the country. Sisters Renee Mueller and Jill Finke host the cottage inn in their hometown of Brenham, and have captured what everyone loves about the South: its charm and warmth. The cottage is located in Brenham, just three blocks from the city's historic downtown with plenty of restaurants, shops, and antiques stores. There are also nearby wineries that make Vintage Southern Comfort a great spot to stay for wine tours.

The 1940s-style cottage can be rented out entirely for a romantic getaway, a girls' trip, or special occasions, giving guests a home away from home for their vacation. There is a full modern kitchen that comes with everything you could possibly need during your stay. The dining room flows into the living room allowing everyone to feel connected, yet not crowded. A master bedroom is available for privacy and features a plush mattress and warm, understated décor. A vintage convertible sofa, daybed, and trundle are offered for extra bedding. The sunlit cottage is furnished with family antiques and heirlooms. Vintage Southern Comfort is sure to suit nearly any travel needs. It's adaptable, warm, and perfectly Southern making you feel more than welcome; you feel at home.

Photographs by Shannon Buck.

612 South Park Street, Brenham, TX 77833
713.826.6915 vintagesoutherncomfort.com

ROCKPORT FULTON

VISIT ROCKPORT FULTON

—

charming Gulf Coast escape with Texas-size heart

The true spirit of Texas can be seen all over this great state, but nowhere more clearly than in Rockport Fulton. Determined, proud, and Texas strong, this small slice of paradise has a big personality. The area suffered some of the most severe damage from Hurricane Harvey in 2017 and responded with a resolve to rebuild, revitalize, and remind everyone why it's the best getaway in Texas.

Located along the Texas Tropical Trail, and a significant stop along the Great Texas Coastal Birding Trail, Rockport Fulton are twin communities nestled among the wind-swept oaks of the Live Oak Peninsula. The towns embody all the charm and hospitality that Texas has to offer and have been a favorite escape for anyone looking for a beach getaway. Accommodations range from quaint bed &

breakfasts to resort-style condos. The region has so much to do, for both adults and children. There are numerous art galleries, city parks, history centers, golf courses, boat cruises, aquariums, scenic piers, a wildlife refuge, and maritime museums. Cool festivals and events are always popping up, so check the schedule online before you go. Plus the nightlife, bars, and restaurants are as good as any big city. Where else could you get fresher seafood?

Photographs courtesy of Rockport-Fulton Chamber of Commerce.

Rockport-Fulton Chamber of Commerce
319 Broadway, Rockport, TX 78382
361.729.6445 rockport-fulton.org

Western Region

Palo Duro Canyon

Photograph by Jim Davis Images.

Cibolo Creek Ranch lakefront guestrooms

Photograph courtesy of City of Marfa.

Hancock Hill behind Sul Ross University in Alpine

Photograph by Cathy McNair.

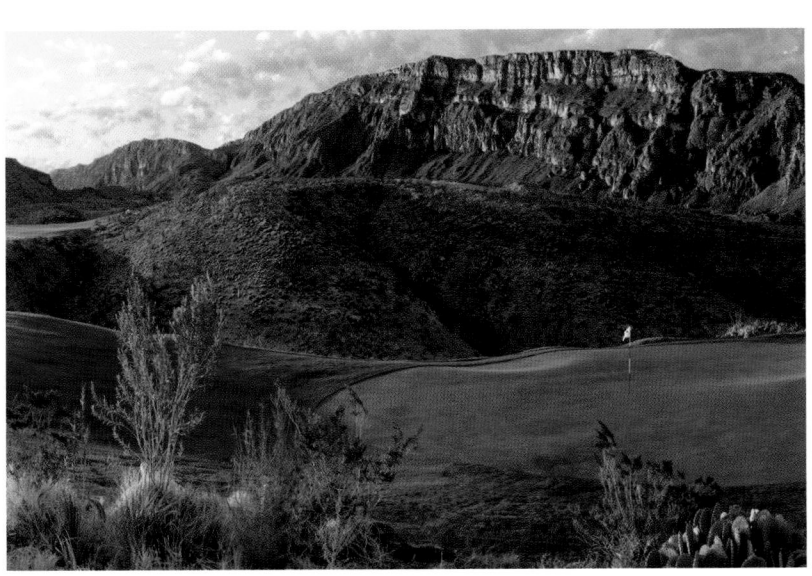

La Jitas golf course
Photograph by Brittany Bay.

Sample Road Trip
Start: Austin
End: Marfa
Miles: 429

Hit the highway early for this road trip to iconic Marfa. If you need caffeine to fuel your adventure, stop at **Open Doors Coffee House** in Johnson City for some of the world's finest coffee beans. Set your map to the small town of Junction for lunch, where you'll find the original **Coopers BBQ**. Get there early for the cabrito—they run out fast. Steer West to Alpine, home of Sul Ross University. While you're there check out the **Museum of The Big Bend**. Their permanent collection of arrowheads, maps and Retablos will impress. After a long day on the road you'll want to check into one of Marfa's funky hotels for a nap. Don't snooze too long though, you won't want to miss the best $5 margarita happy hour around including a rotating menu of small plates from 4 to 6 everyday in **Bar Saint George**. Located in the **Saint George** hotel lobby, **Marfa Book Company** offers a unique selection of books. Try **Jett's Grill** for their incredible chicken-fried sirloin steak with a grilled jalapeño. After a gluttonous night, you'll want to start your day with a healthy juice at **Marfa Squeeze**. Spend your first afternoon in town hitting the galleries and museums. If you are feeling extra adventurous, check out **Marfa Gliders** for a bird's-eye view of the area. You'll want one of those $5 margaritas after the ride.

Cibolo Creek Ranch is right down the road, just 15 miles from the Mexican border. You won't want to leave this peaceful property. Enjoy hiking, fishing, paddle boating, and more. Golf enthusiasts might like **La Jitas Golf Resort**, tucked away in Texas' historic Big Bend. You'll be as busy as you want to be at either of these unique, rugged desert resorts, rich in Old West history.

spotlight

HIGH PLAINS WINE

Llano Estacado has been creating wines of distinction that capture the true essence of Texas since 1976. With warm days and cool nights, the location on the Texas High Plains provides the perfect climate for growing premium wine grapes. Combine that with the master craftsmanship of the winemakers and it's easy to see why Llano Estacado's wines have won more than 1,000 national and international awards. Enjoy the wine. There is something for every occasion and dish. Whether you're throwing a party, grilling for a backyard barbecue, or preparing a five-course tasting menu, Llano Estacado has a wine to complement your food.

LLANO ESTACADO
3426 East FM 1585, Lubbock, TX 79404
800.634.3854   llanowine.com

Photographs courtesy of Llano Estacado.

The McPherson family has been a part of winemaking in Texas for more than 50 years. McPherson Cellars was established in 2000 in homage to Dr. Clinton McPherson, winemaker Kim McPherson's father. Doc McPherson, a pioneer of the modern Texas wine industry, planted experimental vineyards as a chemistry professor at Texas Tech and co-founded the first post-prohibition Texas winery in 1976. Kim studied winemaking at UC Davis and worked in California before returning in 1980 to work with his father. In 2008, he converted Lubbock downtown's 1930s-era Coca-Cola bottling plant into a winery and McPherson Cellars Winery & Tasting Room opened that fall. The tasting room is comfortable and convivial—much like the wines—to be enjoyed with good friends, family, and food. The winery focuses on varieties that thrive in the West Texas climate and soils, all sourced from the Texas High Plains AVA.

MCPHERSON CELLARS WINERY

1615 Texas Avenue, Lubbock, TX 79401

806.687.9463 mcphersoncellars.com

Photographs by Kailee King Photography.

spotlight
MARFA

Marfa, the county seat of Presidio County, is at the junction of US Highway 90 and 67 in far West Texas. It was established in 1883 as a water stop and freight headquarters for the Galveston, Harrisburg, and San Antonio Railway. Fittingly named after a character in a novel, Marfa has a history of attracting creative spirits. Reportedly, the wife of a railroad executive suggested the name Marfa from Fyoder Dostoyevsky's "The Brothers Karamazov," which she was reading at the time.

Marfa is well known for its place in the art world. The Chinati Foundation/La Fundación Chinati is a world class contemporary art museum based upon the ideas of its founder and artist Donald Judd, but you won't find a gallery district. Rather you'll find sprawling beauty that defies any single definition or interpretation. It may be called minimalism, but the implications are anything but minimal. Simple and ever expansive all at once, Marfa's internationally renowned artworks are inextricably linked with the breathtaking West Texas landscape. Dining and nightlife is equally as appealing, as Marfa features everything from tasty dives to fine dining spots. You'll also find charming coffee shops, bakeries, and bars to wet your whistle. Start discovering at visitmarfa.com or 432.729.4772.

Photographs courtesy of the City of Marfa.

Barren beauty in West Texas

Unexpected art is everywhere in Marfa

Texas charm at every turn

Architectural gems

Never short on live entertainment

spotlight
MARFA

El Cosmico is a 21-acre nomadic hotel and campground. In keeping with the belief that life should be a balance of adventure and do-nothingness, it offers shelter, occasional entertainment, opportunity for learning, and access to the majesty of the high plains desert. From its wide open spaces to the vast canopy of stars above, El Cosmico provides temporary liberation from the built world. It is a second home to intrepid travelers and wanderers from all corners of the planet. Accommodations at El Cosmico include renovated vintage trailers, safari and scout tents, Sioux-style teepees, a Mongolian yurt, and tent campsites. The property also offers several communal spaces for guests: a hammock grove, outdoor kitchen, and more.

EL COSMICO
802 South Highland Avenue, Marfa, Texas 79843
432.729.1950 elcosmico.com

Photographs courtesy of the City of Marfa..

Charming and historic, Hotel Paisano offers 41 single rooms and suites, a seasonally heated pool, extensive gift shop and art gallery, a movie memorabilia room, ballroom and conference space, fitness center, and a casual restaurant and lounge with relaxing courtyard seating. It's also a social hub for the area, an oasis for travelers, and a fun West Texas destination. In 1955 Warner Brothers chose Mafa as the location for the filming of the classic film, "Giant." In June of that year the cast and crew, including James Dean, Elizabeth Taylor, and Rock Hudson, made the hotel their headquarters.

HOTEL PAISANO

207 North Highland Avenue, Marfa, Texas 79843

432.729.3669 hotelpaisano.com

Photographs courtesy of the City of Marfa.

spotlight
MARFA

Hotel Saint George is a genuine Marfa endeavor, immersed in local character with the creativity and vision of the people who call this town home. Steeped in the history and culture of Marfa, the hotel stands on the site of the original Hotel Saint George, built in 1886. Step into the lobby and you'll see locally sourced elements and repurposed materials from the building's 1929 incarnation, including original concrete floors, salvaged brick walls, reclaimed marble surfaces, and steel doors and counters, all melded with contemporary works by locally relevant artists. The hotel is also well known for Laventure, the comfortably elegent restaurant helmed by award-winning executive chef Allison Jenkins.

HOTEL SAINT GEORGE

105 South Highland Avenue, Marfa, Texas 79843
432.729.3700 marfasaintgeorge.com

Photographs courtesy of the City of Marfa.

The Thunderbird Hotel was built in 1955, and doesn't look its age. Almost a tribute to modern art, original works adorn its walls, and the gift shop is a must-see. Choose from several rooms in the one and two-story wings. Wrap yourself in Peruvian blankets and admire the funky décor, including cool cowhide rugs on the floor. Treat yourself to a massage, or choose to spend your evening watching the beautiful sunset while seated in the outdoor meeting area. You can also borrow a movie from the DVD library or simply take a walk around town under the star-filled sky.

THUNDERBIRD HOTEL

600 West San Antonio Street, Marfa, Texas 79843

432.729.1984 thunderbirdmarfa.com

Photographs courtesy of the City of Marfa.

DOVES REST CABINS

—

rustic retreat in the scenic panhandle

Doves Rest Cabins, situated in the heart of the Texas Panhandle, offers luxury cabin rentals to intrepid travelers with views of Palo Duro Canyon. You'll quickly escape to another world as the canyon embodies Texas' sense of place and spirit like no other spot on earth. Surrounded by a treasured, iconic symbol of the American Southwest, Doves Rest Cabins is a place to nurture your soul and spirit with natural beauty and quietness.

The Texas Panhandle is the perfect place to get a big taste of Texas even if you only have a small amount of time. From canyons to Cadillacs, and gigantic steaks to grand scenery, the cities of Amarillo and Canyon are an Old West enthusiast's dream. One of the country's best collections of Western art and artifacts can be found at the Panhandle-Plains Historical Museum in Canyon. Mosey on over to the Amarillo Livestock Auction to mingle with real cowboys as they go about the business of buying and selling cattle. For those with interests that are more modern, the city of Amarillo boasts a great art museum and beautiful botanical gardens. If you're traveling with kids, don't miss the thrilling rides at Wonderland Park.

Photographs by Jim Davis Images.

Canyon, TX 972.880.3600
dovesrestcabins.com

NAZARETH

YELLOW ROSE INN

—

small-town plains getaway

If you love exploring small Texas towns and taking in all they have to offer, Nazareth is a find. Located in the central panhandle, the town was built and established by German immigrants at the turn of the century. Those European roots are still evident today with German descendants making up a sizable community in the quiet town. This includes innkeepers Marlene and Dale Acker, and Chanlar and Amanda Osmanski. The two couples run the Victorian-style Yellow Rose Inn and welcome travelers from all over the country. Charming, quiet, and undeniably warm, the inn is ideal for watching sunsets on the veranda and visiting with locals. Ask any guests who've stayed at the inn and they'll tell you that the best part of the visit was the people they met and the conversations they had.

Accommodations include a range of rooms to suit your needs—everything from the refined Northern Lights room to the rustic Brockman Hardware cabin. With a big country breakfast offered in the morning, Yellow Rose gives visitors little reason to leave the inn during their trip. If you're the exploring type, however, Nazareth has a few things to offer that travelers will enjoy: museum tours, gun collectors' displays, farm and dairy tours, and good old-fashioned star gazing at night.

Photograph courtesy of Yellow Rose Inn.

211 Third Street, Nazareth, TX 79063
806.945.2356 yellowroseinntx.com

Destinations to Explore

The Vintage Round Top vacation home
Photography by Haylei Smith.

Villaggio Del Vino in Tyler
Photography by Sam Smead.

Vaudeville at sundown
Photography by Blake Mistich.

Sample Road Trip
Start: Lakeway
End: Fredricksburg
Miles: 76

Lake Travis is a popular attraction for tourists and locals. There are a variety of accommodation options including **Lakeway Resort and Spa** or beautiful lakeview home rentals on **VRBO.com**. Wherever you stay on the lake, you'll find relaxing dining spots like **Canyon Grille** in Lakeway or the famous **Oasis** restaurant—both with breathtaking lake views. A perfect place to take a selfie! On your way to Fredericksburg you'll want to stop at **Stone House Vineyards** in Spicewood for what many think is one of the best wineries in Texas. Enjoy your wine with a cheese plate on the patio overlooking Lake Travis. Take a leisurely drive through the Hill Country to Fredericksburg before checking into your cabin at **Cotton Gin Lodging** or your charming room at **Hoffman Haus**.

You'll have no problem finding wineries to visit in the area, it's the "Napa Valley of Texas." Fredericksburg is also home to many historical sites that tell the stories of German settlers in the Texas Hill Country. You'll find a nice variety of restaurants serving authentic German food around town, like **Otto's**. Don't miss shopping the hip showroom at **Vaudeville**, a curation of rare objects, furniture, décor, accessories, jewelry, and artifacts. If you get hungry while shopping, sit down in the bistro for some new American comfort food.

Spa lounge at Lakeway Resort & Spa
Photography by Lakeway Resort & Spa.

THE SPUR HOTEL

—

down the road from ordinary

Originally built in 1928, the Spur Hotel was renovated and preserved in 1990 and reopened as a boutique hotel. It has been listed among the state's top 10 small hotels and is one of the few historic hotels left on the panhandle plains. Year-round, the Spur plays host to all kinds of visitors: book enthusiasts browsing Larry McMurtry's stores, guests of the famous Royal Theater, attendees of workshops and retreats, hunters from all over the country, business travelers, and families. To learn more, visit thespurhotel.com.

Photographs by Sarah Junek.

VISIT BIG SPRING

—

a multitude of cultural, sporting, and recreational events

Located in central West Texas, Big Spring delivers a mixture of yesterday, today, and tomorrow and welcomes natives and newcomers alike. Home of friendly residents, beautiful landscapes, and a comfortable climate, Big Spring has tons of cultural, sporting and recreational events. It's an ideal place to call home, where you can find friendly folks, great fun, and a beautiful beginning. Start your journey at mybigspring.com.

Photographs by Bruce Schooler of Red Barn Studios.

VISIT BRENHAM

—

in the heart of the Bluebonnet country

In the heart of Texas bluebonnet country is Brenham, a special place that embodies Texas history, culture, and natural beauty. Located in Washington County halfway between Houston and Austin, the town is a friendly, authentic community with plenty of options for you to reconnect with nature, your family, and yourself. Don't miss the local wineries, stunning bluebonnets, Blue Bell ice cream headquarters, and historical sites. All of this—plus the small-town charm—will keep you coming back year after year. Learn more at visitbrenhamtexas.com.

Photographs courtesy of the Washington County Chamber of Commerce — Convention & Visitors Bureau.

SOUTHERN SERENITY RANCH & RETREAT

—

serene Colonial bed & breakfast

Southern Serenity Ranch & Retreat is a fully gated 1929 Colonial on 31 acres with a pictur-esque pond. The Main House boasts more than 6,000 square feet of living space, with seven bedrooms and four-and-a-half bathrooms. With two bedrooms and two bathrooms, the quaint cottage gives visitors 1,150 square feet of space. Both accommodations are furnished with antiques, all-white bedding, and have scenic views of the pond. You'll love the large front porches—perfect for your morning cup of coffee or your evening glass of wine.

Photographs by Melissa Markle.

BLISSWOOD BED & BREAKFAST

—

enjoy the simple life in calming surroundings

BlissWood Bed & Breakfast is located at Lehmann Legacy Ranch, a 500-acre working ranch just an hour west of Houston. Spend a day, a week, or longer in this peaceful country setting with your choice of accommodations—there's a mix of 12 different houses and cabins. All lodging is private with kitchens, bathrooms, and antique furnishings. Enjoy a Texas sunset while you sip refreshments on your front porch and unwind next to the majestic live oaks. Visit blisswood.net.

Photographs by Jumping Rock Photos, Inc.

W HAUS DÉCOR & MORE

—

beautiful boutique on Cedar Creek Lake

W Haus Décor & More is just an hour drive from Dallas—and well worth the trip. A charming boutique, W Haus Décor & More has brought a touch of class to Cedar Creek Lake. Shop the one-of-a-kind selections featuring jewelry, handbags, wraps, and European home décor with Austrian flair. Equally beautiful, The W Haus & Gardens will welcome you into the grand entrance of the region's finest art gallery. It's an ideal venue for small gatherings and celebratory get-togethers. Learn more at whausdecor.com.

Photographs by Jamye Montgomery.

CAMP COMFORT

—

modern sophistication meets summer camp

Built in 1860 in Comfort, Texas, Camp Comfort was originally a bowling alley and has been converted into a non-hosted boutique bed & breakfast on Cypress Creek. Guests can relax with their favorite beverage around the fire pit in the courtyard, or enjoy a wonderful selection from the fresh, organic breakfast options. Snacks are served at the historic social hall each morning, including coffee, juice, tea, muffins, breads, preserves, fruits, and granola. Sound like fun? Start planning your summer camping getaway at camp-comfort.com.

Photographs courtesy of Camp Comfort.

194

FALL CREEK VINEYARDS

—

lush two-bedroom private inn at a beautiful winery

The Fall Creek Vineyards Wine Country Inn is just steps away from the Winery of Fall Creek Vineyards at Driftwood. Here, you can enjoy a glass of the Terrior Reflection series or Classic Fall Creek labels that pair perfectly with gourmet bites from the chef. Gather around the fire with friends on wintery days, or soak in the Texas sun on the patio and porches during the summer. No matter the season, you can relax in the warm comfort of the inn's Southern hospitality. Visit fcv.com to plan your visit.

Photographs courtesy of Fall Creek Vineyards.

THE HANGAR HOTEL

—

relax in the romance of the 1940s

Don't be fooled by the name—The Hangar Hotel is not just for pilots. Built new from the ground up, the Hangar Hotel was uniquely designed with an exterior appearance of a World War II hangar from the 1940s. The hotel has gone beyond conventional design by combining fine woods, granite, custom carpet and tile, and unique furnishings, all with meticulous attention to detail. Guests can relax with an aviation-themed backdrop and enjoy top-notch service, all steeped in the romance and excitement of a bygone era. Plan your visit at hangarhotel.com.

Photograph courtesy of The Hangar Hotel.

WALKER MANOR BED & BREAKFAST

—

a bed & breakfast full of Southern grace

Walker Manor Bed & Breakfast sits in the Historic Main Street District of Gladewater with its charming red brick streets. Known as the antique capital of east Texas, the bed and breakfast, a recorded Texas landmark, is within walking distance of shops, restaurants, a museum, and the famous Gladewater Opry. Beautiful gardens and inviting porches will entice you to stay a while. The innkeepers bring an elegant Southern charm to the place that speaks of a more refined time. Indulge in the elegance and experience a bygone era. Learn more at walkermanortx.com.

Photographs by Pickled Tink Photography.

COUNTRY WOODS INN

—

an adventurous taste of the rural life

Welcome to an adventure. Discover the beauty of your family again at Country Woods Inn. Walk the trails on 40 wooded acres along the Paluxy River where you can fish and swim. Sleep like you have never slept before in a 100-year-old-farm house or vintage Airstream. Stay in a Santa Fe Rail Car, cabin, or the Main Lodge for groups of up to 60 people. Country Woods Inn is the perfect setting for family reunions, church retreats, and weddings. Be sure to check out the Chapel in the Woods as well.

Photographs by Melissa Willis (top) and courtesy of Country Woods Inn (all others).

INN ON THE RIVER

—

historic, boutique bed & breakfast meets corporate venue

The meticulously restored inn offers fine dining, personalized service, romantic getaways, or corporate retreats, all just a short drive from Dallas and Fort Worth. Glen Rose is a favorite touring destination for car and motorcycle clubs. The inn, with its secluded parking, is a great location to host your next event. It's a place where the steady stream of interruptions and grating city traffic is replaced by a gently flowing river and sounds of birds singing. Plan your visit at innontheriver.com.

Photographs by Mission Street Photography.

CITY OF JEFFERSON

—

a town with an ever-evolving story

There are many ways to experience and enjoy the cultural heritage of Jefferson. Whether it's a ride aboard the steam engine, a tour through one of the many museums, a horse-drawn carriage ride, or shopping and dining, there are plenty of ways for visitors to connect with the story of Jefferson. The town wants to share its modern-day appeal as well as a charming Texas hot spot with a high quality of life and tons of things to do. See what it has to offer at visitjeffersontexas.com.

Photographs by Hollis Shadden.

THE BOARDWALK INN

—

a seaside getaway in the middle of it all

Nestled in the heart of the Kemah Boardwalk, The Boardwalk Inn offers spectacular waterfront views and relaxing seaside charm. Just steps from the endless entertainment and outstanding dining of the boardwalk, the boutique hotel features 56 guestrooms, including four luxury suites. Each room has updated interiors and a balcony overlooking the plaza and amusements. Start planning your getaway at kemahboardwalkinn.com.

Photographs by Landry's Inc.

DEER LAKE LODGE RESORT & HEALTH SPA

—

self-directed detox programs

Deer Lake Lodge Resort & Health Spa offers colonics, raw food and liquid fasting, cbd oil, energy work, chiropractic care, yoga, iridology, reiki, hypnotherapy, therapeutic spa treatments, and so much more. Set in a rustic-chic environment, the resort and spa is one of the first of its kind and offers a multi-faceted cleansing program. Hidden among 50 acres of tall pines and live creeks, your secret escape awaits. It's only a short drive from Houston and The Woodlands. Get all the details at deerlakelodge.com.

Photographs courtesy of Deer Lake Lodge.

RANCHO PILLOW

—

there's nothing quite like this magical retreat

Set among the farms and ranches of southeast Texas, Rancho Pillow is a whimsical wonderland that is a true artistic adventure for visitors. The 20-acre compound is nestled near the tiny art town of Round Top and the entire acreage and its dwellings are available to rent. What began as a family compound in 2006 has become a heartfelt landscape that welcomes everyone. Poetic and playful, it's an idyllic shelter for Latin American folk-art finds, colorful architectural restorations, and collected curiosities. It's simply magical. Learn more at ranchopillow.com.

Photographs by Knoxy Knox.

STONE HOUSE VINEYARD

—

luxury destination winery with an Australian heritage

The name Stone House Vineyard suggests permanence and durability, two qualities that owner Angela Moench undoubtedly espouses in her winemaking and grape growing. Angela hails from the Barossa Valley wine country in Australia and continues to source grapes and winemaking techniques from that area. This results in wines that blend Texas and Australian methodologies and flavors to showcase two burgeoning viticultural regions. An enthusiasm about good wine and food permeates everything here; you'll want to bring family and friends. Plan your visit at stonehousevineyard.com.

Photographs by Angela Moench.

THE WOODLANDS RESORT

—

luxury resort nestled in the forest

A world of intoxicating beauty awaits, just 30 minutes from downtown Houston. Tucked away in the Texas Piney Woods on 28,000 acres of natural forest, The Woodlands Resort & Conference Center is an ideal vacation destination for families, friends, and couples, as well as an exceptional venue for meetings, conferences, social events, and weddings. The 406 well-appointed guest rooms offer all the comforts of home and feature captivating views of lakes, dazzling pools, or tree-lined fairways. Learn more at thewoodlandsresort.com.

Photographs by Stewart Cohen Pictures.

INDEX OF PROPERTIES

Signature
Boutique Books

SPECTACULAR TEXAS
OUTDOOR LIVING

LUSH LANDSCAPES AND STYLISH SPACES
Jolie Carpenter

SPECTACULAR WINERIES
of Texas

A CAPTIVATING TOUR OF ESTABLISHED, ESTATE AND BOUTIQUE WINERIES

EXPERIENCE AUSTIN
& THE HILL COUNTRY

THE AREA'S MOST UNIQUE AND INTERESTING PLACES

SPECTACULAR KITCHENS TEXAS

INSPIRING KITCHEN AND DINING SPACES
Jolie Carpenter

LUXURY HOMES

AN EXCLUSIVE SHOWCASE OF TEXAS' FINEST ARCHITECTS & BUILDERS
Jolie Carpenter

Beautiful Weddings
of Texas

CELEBRATION INSPIRATION
Jolie Carpenter

DREAM HOMES
of TEXAS

AN EXCLUSIVE SHOWCASE OF TEXAS' FINEST ARCHITECTS AND BUILDERS
by Jolie Carpenter

BEAUTIFUL BEDROOMS & BATHS
of Texas

Jolie Carpenter

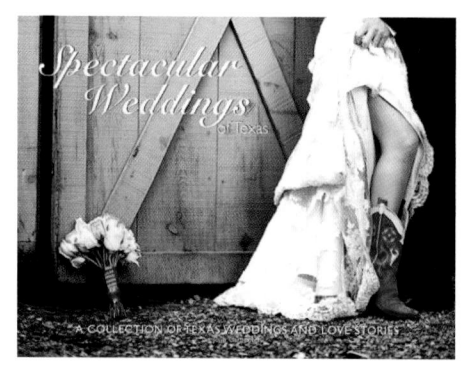

Spectacular Weddings
of Texas

A COLLECTION OF TEXAS WEDDINGS AND LOVE STORIES

SPECTACULAR HOMES
of Texas

AN EXCLUSIVE SHOWCASE OF TEXAS' FINEST DESIGNERS

Beautiful Homes
of Texas

AN EXCLUSIVE COLLECTION OF THE FINEST DESIGNERS IN TEXAS

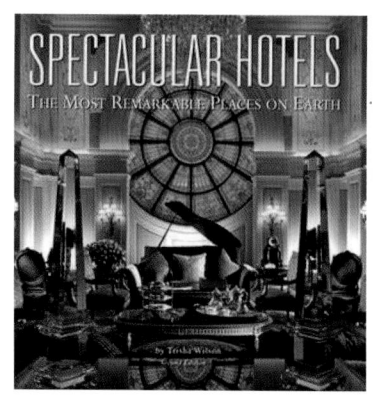

SPECTACULAR HOTELS
THE MOST REMARKABLE PLACES ON EARTH

by Trisha Wilson

SPECTACULAR RESTAURANTS
of Texas